A Notre Dame Man
THE MIKE DeCICCO STORY

CORBY BOOKS wishes to acknowledge the generous sponsorship of this book provided by the 1966 National Champions Charitable Fund. Special thanks go to Ron Jeziorski, Dan Harshman and Brian Boulac. We are also grateful to The University of Notre Dame Archives, the Notre Dame Sports Information Office and the DeCicco family for generous assistance in providing graphics. Special thanks for financial support and many contributions to John and Wendy Bognar and Don and Susie Laurie.

A Notre Dame Man
THE MIKE DeCICCO STORY

BY JEREMY D. BONFIGLIO

Foreword by
REV. THEODORE M. HESBURGH, C.S.C.,
PRESIDENT EMERITUS OF THE UNIVERSITY OF NOTRE DAME

A NOTRE DAME MAN:
The Mike DeCicco Story

10 9 8 7 6 5 4 3 2

ISBN: 978-0-9890731-7-2

Distributed by ACTA Publications
4848 N. Clark Street, Chicago, IL 60640
www.actapublications.com

Published by
CORBY BOOKS
A Division of Corby Publishing, LP
P.O. Box 93
Notre Dame, IN 46556
Editorial Office (574) 784-3482

Manufactured in the United States of America

For my father, James, and my son, William

CONTENTS

FOREWORD

AT THE UNIVERSITY OF NOTRE DAME, students who participate in intercollegiate athletics must be more than football or basketball players. They must be more than their position on the field or the court. They must be students in the classroom as well as students of the game.

There is great value in athletic participation. Young men and women are confronted by basic life values as they compete individually and collectively against their opponents. Such experiences provide strong opportunities for self-knowledge. It's one of the reasons athletics are important at Notre Dame. Academic achievement, however, is more important. To play here at Notre Dame you must consider yourself a student first, which is why we always refer to our young men and women as student-athletes.

Notre Dame's admissions and academic standards are rigorous. While a considerable number of our student-athletes have the ability and skills needed to achieve academic success without assistance, the demands of practice schedules, game preparations and travel can be overwhelming for those who have not developed effective study skills.

That became most apparent in the spring of 1963, when five members of the Notre Dame football program flunked out. That's when I, along with executive vice president Rev. Edmund P. Joyce, determined we that would try to avoid the same type of experience from occurring again.

We needed to establish a strong academic advisory program for student-athletes beyond the purview of the athletic department. This new department would report directly to Ned Joyce, but we needed someone to oversee the program who was knowledgeable about sports and academics; someone who was a leader and could walk in both worlds.

That someone was Mike DeCicco.

Mike was a member of the engineering faculty as well as the head fencing coach at Notre Dame. His academic-advising program would prove to be a pioneering effort in the field, which is reflected in the consistent graduation rate of more than 98 percent of our student-athletes these past 40 years.

Some people are just made for the job. Mike DeCicco was made for this one. He established study skills practice and both individual and group tutoring sessions. He emphasized deeds over words, and actions over talk. He emphasized self-responsibility as well as responsibility to family and teammates. His devotion to his own family, to Jesus and the Blessed Virgin Mary, the patroness of Notre Dame, served as a constant example. He did this all while leading his fencing teams to five National Championships, becoming the winningest coach in the 125-year history of Notre Dame athletics.

If you're a man of faith, you bring honesty and integrity and dedication to a cause. Mike DeCicco had all of those things. You could always be sure that he was on the side of the angels. He was Notre Dame to the core. He always stood for what was right, and we were very lucky to have him.

Rev. Theodore M. Hesburgh, C.S.C.
President Emeritus
University of Notre Dame

INTRODUCTION

IN THE SPRING OF 1963, the University of Notre Dame football program was reeling.

Joe Kuharich's Irish were still smarting from their third 5-5 season in four years, which seemed almost remarkable given the dismal 2-8 season of 1960 that included a school-record, eight-game losing streak.

The Irish hadn't had a winning season since 1958 when the Terry Brennan era ended with a 6-4 record, and it was clear, even then, that this would be one of the worst stretches in the storied history of Notre Dame football.

By March of '63, Kuharich had had enough, resigning as head coach to assume the post of supervisor of officials in the NFL. Because it was already spring, Notre Dame asked freshman football coach and assistant athletic director Hugh Devore to step in as interim head coach while the search for a permanent replacement was being conducted.

Devore, after all, had been an interim coach at Notre Dame once before. When Frank Leahy entered the U.S. Navy in 1944 and Edward McKeever left for Cornell University in

March 1945, it was Devore who took his place, leading the Irish to a 7–2–1 mark before Leahy returned the following year.

This time, however, Devore's mission was as much about keeping the program afloat and keeping recruiting alive as it was about winning games. The 1963 team didn't have the talent to be as competitive as DeVore's 1945 team. The depth chart only got thinner when, heading into practice in the spring of '63, the Irish learned that five Notre Dame football players had failed to meet the University's minimum academic standards and would not be returning in the fall. This caught the attention of Rev. Theodore M. Hesburgh, Notre Dame's president, and Rev. Edmund P. Joyce, his executive vice president. That's when the two men began discussing the need to create a new academic-advising program for student-athletes, starting with the Irish football team.

The timing was ideal. A search committee, under Hesburgh and Joyce, was already seeking a new, long-term head football coach who could win games as well as graduate players. This, however, wasn't public knowledge, and in '63 it may have appeared to those outside Hesburgh's inner circle as if the University, and in particular its president, had given up on the football program altogether. After all, the new 13-story Memorial Library, which was later renamed after Hesburgh, was built on historic Cartier Field where Knute Rockne's teams once played. The library's doors opened in September 1963 while the Notre Dame faithful suffered through Devore's miserable 2-7 season.

Hesburgh was known for his staunch views on academic standards and his stance on Civil Rights, serving as a member of the United States Civil Rights Commission beginning in 1957. What was perhaps less widely known is that Hesburgh was also keenly aware of how television was beginning to change college football.

By 1950, a small number of schools, including Notre Dame, had already entered into individual contracts with networks to broadcast their games regionally. Television had brought renewed exposure to the college game. That may have been a nice selling point in recruiting high school athletes, but it also brought in money, added scrutiny and, with it, a more fervent desire to win at all costs.

Hesburgh suspected, and rightly so, that the money from television would push some universities to loosen their academic standards in the pursuit of the best players, and wins would become more important than degrees earned. Hesburgh and Joyce believed there was a way to maintain high academic standards and still find success in athletic competition. Their solution was academic advising.

From the beginning, creating an academic-advising program was as much about the University maintaining its integrity and standards as it was about keeping its athletes from falling behind in class.

To avoid even the suggestion of impropriety, Hesburgh and Joyce immediately agreed that any oversight into the academic standing of Notre Dame's athletes had to be done outside the scope of its athletic department. First, the new academic advisor would report directly to Joyce and not the athletic director. The academic advisor had to know the University's rules and principles guiding both academics and athletics and be someone who could bridge the gap between students, professors, coaches and administrators. It was a tall order, but after an internal search they found someone who met every standard.

His name was Mike DeCicco.

CHAPTER ONE

The Old Bait and Switch

"Every time a job opens at a university you look first at the people you have. When we did that Mike DeCicco was the obvious choice."
— Rev. Theodore M. Hesburgh, C.S.C.,
Notre Dame President Emeritus

THE CALL CAME ON A THURSDAY. All the important ones usually did. At least that's the way Mike DeCicco remembered it.

It was summer in 1964, a full decade since DeCicco returned to teach at his alma mater and about six years longer than he had planned on staying. It's not that he didn't like South Bend, Indiana. He and his wife Polly had made a nice home on Oakside Street on the city's south side. Their five kids, Linda, Michele, Nick, Della, and Michael Jr., liked it, too. DeCicco, however, was a no-nonsense New Jersey native whose personality was much bigger than his stocky 5-foot-7-inch frame, and this was the Midwest.

His laugh was often at a decibel level that would turn heads, and he wasn't shy about doling out hugs. He could be a stern man, but was fair to those who treated him with respect. If you didn't? Well, he might have a few choice words to say

1

about that. It all made DeCicco a rather colorful bird among the black and white flock at the University of Notre Dame.

Pat Roth, the secretary for Rev. Edmund P. Joyce, was the voice on the other end of the telephone line. DeCicco had been summoned to his office in the Main Building, although he wasn't told why. Before the receiver left his hand, he couldn't help but wonder if his East Coast honesty might have ruffled a few Indiana feathers.

The man affectionately known as Father Ned was second in command at Notre Dame, behind only University President Rev. Theodore M. Hesburgh. So what did Ned Joyce want to discuss with an engineering professor?

DeCicco, however, was more than just another member of the faculty. A year after returning to campus, friend and mentor Walter Langford had finally talked DeCicco into becoming the assistant fencing coach. It was quite an accomplishment considering it took Langford another six years to talk him into taking over for good.

DeCicco had just finished his third season as head coach, and the Irish fencers were beginning to flourish. DeCicco's first season was certainly not indicative of what was to come. His team struggled to a 7-8 finish, but rebounded to a 14-2 record and a 10th-place finish at the NCAA Championships in '63, and 15-2, finishing fifth at the NCAAs in '64.

Among Joyce's responsibilities, DeCicco remembered, was overseeing the athletic department, so Hesburgh could focus more on academics.

"Fencing," DeCicco thought as he looked up at the light flickering off the Golden Dome atop the Main Building. "That must be it."

DeCicco hadn't even sat down in Joyce's office when Father Ned began praising his coaching efforts. While each compliment was heartfelt, Joyce must have come off a bit like a used car salesman getting ready for the old bait and switch, because it wasn't long before both men knew there was something else on Father Ned's mind. DeCicco had been waiting for the other shoe to drop. Then, it did.

"How would you like to start an office of academic advising for student-athletes?" Joyce asked.

DeCicco was dumbfounded. Academic advising for athletes was such a new concept that DeCicco wasn't sure how it would differ from what the University already had in place. He knew that the athletic department tutored a few hard-luck cases, but none of his fencers ever fit that bill. What DeCicco knew about academic advising "could fit into a gnat's fanny." Still, he listened to the pitch.

Joyce revealed to DeCicco what he and Hesburgh had discussed since those five football players flunked out in the spring of '63. Notre Dame athletes must be students working for a degree first, Joyce said, and players second. He also stressed to DeCicco that the integrity of the University must never be compromised.

"Their worry," DeCicco said, "was that, with TV and the money that sports was beginning to draw with sponsors, there would be schools, coaches and athletes who would begin to play games with the athletic programs."

Wins brought television contracts and TV deals brought money. It wasn't a stretch to believe that some schools would bring in athletes who only wanted to play for victories, deals and cash. Wins were just as important at Notre Dame, but not more than academics. Not to Hesburgh. Not to Joyce. Not to DeCicco.

DeCicco, however, was reluctant to take the post himself. His focus was teaching engineering. He had created a laboratory to study thermodynamics, particularly heat transfer and air conditioning, which was not yet widely used. He taught the first air conditioning course at the University and was also an engineering counselor as part of Notre Dame's freshman year of studies program—not to mention his time on the fencing strip. He didn't have time to babysit football players who skipped class.

"They said I'd probably just need to help two or three kids and it wouldn't take much to get it done," DeCicco said. "Well, they didn't know."

DeCicco respected Joyce enough, however, to let the idea ruminate. He told Father Ned he needed some time to think about it, even though he already knew what he thought. He was honored they would ask, but where would he find the time? He was a husband and father, a professor and coach. Joyce didn't say anything about lightening his course load or extra compensation for that matter. What would Polly think?

That was the real question. Later that night, as he had done a million times before and would do a million times after, DeCicco turned to his wife for her insight.

He'd never admit it, at least not in public, but she had always been the sensible one. It was Polly who urged him to return to Indiana and Notre Dame for the teaching position, even though it meant a pay cut. She believed the opportunity trumped the paycheck. Polly usually saw the bigger picture that sometimes eluded him and he needed that insight now.

"I said 'Honey, I've got enough to do now without adding another phase,'" DeCicco recalled. "And she's the one who told me, 'Mike, do you think they will ever ask you to do anything else if you don't volunteer to do this?' And she was right. They needed somebody and I don't know what possessed them to ask me, but they did."

DeCicco called Joyce the next day and said, "I'll do it." It was a job he never asked for or sought out, but it was his now.

CHAPTER TWO

Executive John

"A guy who was deficient in just one subject could have flunked out of school if there hadn't been any attention paid to it. When Mike stepped in it changed their entire life."

— Ara Parseghian, Notre Dame football coach, 1964-74

IN AUGUST 1964, at the beginning of the school year, Mike DeCicco added academic advisor for student-athletes to his list of titles, which already included fencing coach, engineering professor, husband and father.

After coming to terms with his choice, DeCicco was ready to work, but he needed to figure out how he fit into his new role, and just what the position would actually entail. He agreed with Hesburgh and Joyce who thought any oversight into the academic standing of Notre Dame's athletes must be done outside the scope of its athletic department. While Hesburgh and Joyce saw this as a way to avoid any suggestion of impropriety or grade fixing, DeCicco believed that to truly make students accountable, he needed the autonomy to make tough decisions without being overruled by a coach or member of the athletic department staff. That might mean pulling a student from practice, or keeping him out of a game. But how much power would DeCicco actually have?

He brought his concerns to Joyce, who agreed that DeCicco would report directly to him and not the athletic director, eliminating any notion that the athletic department had sway over its athletes' academic standing. DeCicco, however, was a practical man. He knew the difference between appearances and reality.

"My fear was that the coaches would still try to dictate rules for me to follow," DeCicco said. "So I said to Father Joyce, 'You've got to make sure these guys know that when it comes to academics I'm in charge.'"

DeCicco needed autonomy and Joyce would provide it for him. Father Ned outlined the new program for coaches and athletic department officials. DeCicco would be in charge and no coach had the authority to dictate academic rules. No coach could go to any faculty member to discuss the academic performance of any athlete or interfere with DeCicco's methods. If he heard otherwise, they would answer to him.

"If anybody would squeal or say this isn't right," Hesburgh said, "old Ned Joyce was there to sell them very quickly."

The experiment began with the football program under new head coach Ara Parseghian. DeCicco knew that if the program was going to work, Parseghian would have to be on board.

There was already a lot of buzz surrounding the hiring of Parseghian. First, he was not a Notre Dame graduate, as every head coach since Knute Rockne had been. Second, Parseghian was Presbyterian and not Catholic. This fueled the gossip by already impatient alumni about how far their beloved football program had strayed. But Parseghian knew football, and he knew how to win in an environment where academics mattered.

Parseghian, who played two seasons for the Cleveland Browns, launched his coaching career at his alma mater, Miami University in Ohio, as an assistant under Woody Hayes. He was elevated to head coach in 1950 when Hayes went to Ohio State, and in five years compiled a 39-6-1 record. That's when the Big 10, this time Northwestern, came calling for him as well. Northwestern wasn't exactly a football powerhouse, but Parseghian still won more games than he lost in his eight seasons there. After a bit of a falling out with Northwestern's athletic department, Parseghian heard the rumor that Hugh Devore's tenure at Notre Dame was temporary. He called Joyce to see if they were in fact looking for a coach. Joyce confirmed that they were, and Parseghian lobbied for the job. It wasn't a tough sell.

After all, the Wildcats had recently renewed their series with the Irish after a decade-long hiatus, and Parseghian's Northwestern teams defeated Notre Dame four straight seasons.

"I thought, if you can't beat him," Hesburgh said, "you better hire him."

Parseghian's academic track record also seemed to fit with what Hesburgh, Joyce and DeCicco were starting. Both Miami and Northwestern mirrored Notre Dame in academic expectations of its athletes, and Parseghian and his assistants had developed their own informal tutoring system to assist players who had trouble in the Northwestern classroom. So when Father Ned told Parseghian about DeCicco's role, the coach was all for it.

"Northwestern and Notre Dame are very similar in terms of academics," Parseghian said. "The difference is, when I got to Notre Dame I had a little depth, and I also had Mike DeCicco."

DeCicco officially started the program on a Monday. His new office would be in the Main Building, and not with the coaches. The physical separation, he thought, would also help establish the program's autonomy.

"There were offices I could have had in the athletic department, but I wanted to be in the Main Building because when you say you're working for Father Joyce and Father Hesburgh you wanted to be close enough to them that the faculty would respect you."

That first morning, DeCicco went to see Pat Roth, Joyce's secretary, who had the key to his new office. She handed it to DeCicco and directed him to a doorway by the stairs across from the accounting office.

DeCicco opened the door. He could still smell the fresh paint. Real estate was at a premium in the Main Building and his office reflected that. It was small, divided by a thin partition with a couple chairs and an old desk.

"They told me it was Rockne's old desk, but it wasn't much of a desk," DeCicco said. "It wasn't much of an office either. If you were tall enough you could stretch your arms and touch the two walls. But at least the Main Building was my address."

He'd make do. He didn't need much—just a place to make phone calls, a place where students could wait. It would work.

DeCicco was just settling in when he heard someone fidgeting at the door. He let out a boisterous, "Come on in! The door's open."

He was expecting a student. Instead Jim Frick, the Executive Director of the Notre Dame Alumni Association, walked in.

DeCicco knew Frick and was glad to see him. "Hi, Jim. What can I do for you?"

"What the heck is going on in here?" Frick asked.

"Well," DeCicco replied, "this is my office."

Frick was puzzled. "Office? What do you mean this is your office? When I left on Friday this was the executive john."

Suddenly, the size of the room, the fresh paint smell, it all made sense. Just a few days earlier, DeCicco's brand new office in the Main Building—the one he hoped by its proximity to Joyce and Hesburgh would add some respectability to this new academic advising venture—was a hastily converted men's room.

"That moment," DeCicco said, "certainly gave me a hint at how important that job of mine was going to be."

CHAPTER THREE

Pink Slips

"My mother was his sounding board. He'd come home and they would huddle in the kitchen. She kept him focused. She always reminded him what he was doing and why he was doing it."

— Linda DeCicco,
Eldest daughter of Mike and Polly DeCicco

THE FIRST TWO WEEKS of his new job DeCicco spent on the telephone.

He had coached fencing—as an assistant and head coach —for about 10 years now. It was through fencing that he knew, or was at least familiar with, coaches and athletic directors from about 100 other universities. Finding out what they were doing with their own athletes, what had worked for them, and what didn't, certainly felt like a good place to start.

A lot of other fencing coaches were also administrators. In fact, they all had other assignments at their schools so it would be easy for him to find out how they handled student-athletes who weren't making the grade. DeCicco called every athletic director he knew. He even hit up the director of the Big 10, because he'd know what those schools were doing.

"Nobody, nobody was doing anything like this," DeCicco said. "They all told me the same thing—'Oh, we don't need that, our kids are OK.' Well, until I started, I thought the same thing."

The only school where DeCicco found an academic advisor was at the University of Texas, or so he was told by a campus operator. But when he spoke to the man, he was just an assistant football coach whose only real academic role was seeing that the admissions office accepted the players they had recruited.

"Do you do anything once they're in?" DeCicco asked.

"No," the coach responded. "Our kids help themselves."

More than 100 calls later, DeCicco realized he was truly starting from scratch.

"I didn't find one program," he said, "not one program in the entire United States."

Instead of looking outside the University, DeCicco looked at his new charges. He began by familiarizing himself with the names of the football players on the Notre Dame roster. They had all been told by Parseghian and Joyce that DeCicco would be monitoring their academic progress until they graduated.

"Generally, the purpose was to work with them and their professors, department heads and deans," DeCicco said, "giving them all the help they needed to succeed academically."

The first month students were in classes, DeCicco called every football player to ask how they were handling their course load. Often the responses were the same—"Everything is going great, no problem."

Joyce also was checking in, only with DeCicco.

"He'd call me up and say 'How's it going?'" DeCicco recalled. "And I said, 'Father, everything is going great, no problem.'"

One of those conversations, as it turns out, came on another Thursday. DeCicco had been looking through the high school transcripts of a freshman defensive tackle named Alan Page, a former candidate for a National Merit Scholarship. Soon after DeCicco talked with Page, Joyce called.

"And I told him, 'Just today Alan Page came by and he told me that he's doing OK, and most of the kids are saying that,'" DeCicco said. "So maybe this job isn't going to be as difficult as I thought it was going to be in the beginning."

Luckily for DeCicco, there was some academic accountability already in place for all Notre Dame students. The pink-slip system had been used for years, particularly during a student's freshman year. Pink slips were essentially warnings sent out mid-semester to let students and their advisors know that they were in danger of getting a below average grade in a particular class.

It just so happened that those pink slips were handed out on Friday and, when DeCicco walked into his office at 7 a.m. Monday morning, stacked neatly on his desk was a pile of pink slips about an inch thick.

"Holy crap!" DeCicco said. "Where did these come from?"

DeCicco grabbed the stack, and right on top was the name Alan Page. The football team had opened the season at

Wisconsin, and because of the travel day Page missed an exam that he had yet to make up.

"I thought, 'How can that be?'" DeCicco said. "I just talked to Alan and he looked at me and said 'Mr. DeCicco, I know I'm doing at least C work.' The lesson I learned is that these kids always think of what grade they'll end up with, and not what they were doing in the moment."

DeCicco hadn't even flipped through the rest of the pink slips when Pat Roth called.

"Mike," she said. "Do you have some time? Father Joyce would like to see you."

Joyce normally didn't arrive on campus until mid-morning, and it wasn't even 7:30 a.m.

"That's when I put two-and-two together," DeCicco said. "Father Joyce put the pink slips on my desk. Who else would have put Alan Page's pink slip right on top?"

DeCicco scheduled the meeting for later that morning so he could talk to Polly. She, after all, was partly responsible for his predicament since she talked him into the job in the first place.

"Polly, I'm going to have the shortest academic-advising assignment in history," he told her.

"And why's that?" she said. DeCicco explained how he asked each student how he was doing and that every one of them said they were OK.

"Well, that's stupid to ask the kids," Polly said. "Look at our own kids. Ask any of them and they will tell you the same thing.

'I'm doing all right, Ma. No problem.' You've got to do what we do. You've got to meet with the teachers."

Polly was right, again, but how could DeCicco meet with every faculty member? He needed a new system. On the back of an envelope he scribbled a list of questions to ask each professor:

- What is the grade level student X has in class thus far?
- Is the student attending and attentive in class?
- Does the student need any outside help, namely a tutor?
- And can you recommend a tutor for the student?

Those four questions would be prefaced by, "In order to assist this student to successfully meet the requirements for your class and with the permission of your dean and provost of this university, would you be kind enough to respond to the following questions."

When DeCicco met with Joyce later that morning, he was armed with a solution.

"So, what did you think of the pink slip list?" Joyce asked.

"I already have Alan Page coming in today," DeCicco replied.

DeCicco then showed Joyce the envelope with his idea for monitoring student-athletes. The two men agreed that it could be the answer, and Joyce assured DeCicco that he would see to it that the professors, the deans and the provost would support him.

DeCicco knew what that meant. The only person who

had that kind of authority was Father Hesburgh. And Joyce was about to ask him to implement a campus-wide academic policy based on a questionnaire he scribbled on the back of an envelope.

It had better work, DeCicco thought, or soon he might get a pink slip of his own.

CHAPTER FOUR

A Better Life

"I was raised in the Depression, but don't ask me about the Depression because I had all I could eat and drink."

— Mike DeCicco, Notre Dame academic advisor, 1964-92

MICHAEL ANTHONY DECICCO was born Nov. 16, 1927, in Newark, New Jersey.

His father, Nicola, worked first on the Lackawanna Railroad as part of William Truesdale's rebuilding program, which included the 28-mile cutoff straight across western New Jersey between Slateford and Port Morris junctions; and then as a crane operator for Martin Dennis Company, a division of Diamond Alkali, moving the chrome ore off ships that came from Africa all the way up the Hudson River to the factory town of Kearny, New Jersey.

His mother, Della, was a seamstress, creating tailor-made suits for Rogers Peet, the New York City men's clothing company whose reputation as one of the finer things in life made its way into the song "Marry the Man Today" from "Guys and Dolls."

Both Nick and Della were Italian immigrants who came to America, like so many others, in search of a better life. The greatest surge of Italian immigration took place between 1880 and 1920, bringing more than 4 million Italians to America's shores. About 80 percent of those immigrants came from Southern Italy, especially from Sicily, Campania, Abruzzo and Calabria, following the stiff economic measures imposed on the South after Italian unification in 1861.

America needed manual labor, and Italian immigrants needed jobs. The men became heavily involved in public works—such as the construction of roads, sewers, subways and bridges—being carried out at the time in the northeastern cities. The women most frequently worked as seamstresses in the garment industry or worked at home.

Nick arrived first, in 1924, when he was 19 years old. In Pratola Serra in the province of Avellino, about 42 miles east of Naples, he had grown close to the Petrettas family who had helped his mother raise him during Italy's lean years. Shortly after the Petrettas men came to New Jersey, they sponsored Nick's own immigration, and he lived with them after arriving in Newark.

Della came to America a short time later with her parents, Guiseppe and Brigida DeVincenzo, her sister, Laura, 16, and her brother, Pat, 12. Della was the oldest at 18. They were sharecroppers from Pescopagano in the province of Potenza, about 83 miles east of Naples, and came for the familiar promise of "streets paved with gold" as advertised in pamphlets dropped throughout the Italian countryside.

It was that shared dream that put Nick in a room with

Della for the first time an ocean away from where they were born. Nick had come to the DeVincenzo home to visit Della's father, Guiseppe, who also had worked on the Lackawanna Railroad.

The 6-foot-2, blue-eyed and broad-shouldered Nick had a natural swagger that came with a Gary Cooper bravado. Some people in the neighborhood called him "The Sheik" for his resemblance to movie star Rudolph Valentino.

The petite Della had had her share of boyfriends by then. She left one behind in Italy, and was dating a young man in Brooklyn, New York, when Nick caught her eye.

"My dad came in the room wearing a red sweater looking tall, blond and handsome," Mike DeCicco said. "That was all she needed to fall in love with him."

It also helped that Nick scared her Brooklyn boyfriend off by exercising a little of that swagger. But she didn't seem to mind.

They got married twice—once at the justice of the peace and two weeks later at the altar, at St. Lucy's Church on Feb. 20, 1927. They rented a three-room apartment at 20 Mount Prospect Avenue, in the city's First Ward, where Mike DeCicco, the couple's first and only child, was born. The DeVincenzos, and Della's younger brother, Pat, lived next door at 18 Mount Prospect Avenue. The close proximity was good for Mike, who spent much of the week with his grandparents while his parents worked late, making the necessary sacrifices for a better life. Both his grandmother and grandfather nurtured in him a love for all things scholarly, which he carried with him the rest of his life.

"My grandfather wrote letters, in Italian, for men who were working in Newark and could not read or write," DeCicco said. "He used the classic Italian script, and he was able to say the entire Mass in Latin in front of an altar he had in his bedroom."

Nick would get up at 4 a.m. to walk to work and back to save the five-cent fare. While working on the Lackawanna Railroad, he would carry home on his shoulder a railroad tie until he made a pile big enough for him and his brother-in-law Pat to saw into firewood and burn with their coal. Della, meanwhile, brought home scraps of material from Rogers Peet to sew collars and sleeves long into the night. Their work ethic, and a little luck, kept them both employed through the Great Depression, and shielded their son from some of the worst hardships.

By 1940, that hard work began to pay off, and Nick and Della had saved enough money to buy their own home at 244 Ridge Street, just off Bloomfield Avenue.

At the time, Newark was divided into sections, each occupied by a different ethnic group. The Ironbound section or East Ward, bound by the railroad, was predominantly Polish. The Weequahic section of Newark was mostly Jewish. The Sicilians settled (for the most part) on 14th Avenue. Another colony of Italians inhabited the Silver Lake district, which spilled over from the northern edge of Newark into Belleville.

The First Ward, whose neighborhood touchstone was St. Lucy's Church, was mostly made up of Italians from the province of Avellino. It was bounded in the south by the tracks of the Lackawanna Railroad, in the west by Branch Brook Park, in the north by Bloomfield and Fourth avenues, and in the east by the Passaic River and Broad Street.

Almost all the merchants in Newark spoke Italian in their neighborhoods—even Jewish grocer Philip Myer, DeCicco remembers. "I thought he was Italian because he spoke our language."

Italian was also spoken at home. DeCicco did not speak English until he went to McKinley Grade School, where he modeled his parents and worked hard, too. In 1940, he was valedictorian of his class at McKinley, even though most of his Saturdays were spent helping his parents around the house.

"We'd clean the whole house, open all the windows, clean the windows and floors every week," DeCicco said. "Then Sunday afternoons we'd go to a movie after the noon meal."

DeCicco went with his father for cartoons and the serials —Flash Gordon, The Lone Ranger—during the occasional Saturday matinee, and with both parents on Sundays to see the films with Clark Gable and Douglas Fairbanks. Della also never missed "Dish Night" on Wednesdays, taking her son to the Colonial Theater on Bloomfield Avenue, for the theater's promotional free dinner plate to complete her set.

Just around the corner on Bloomfield was Ferraro's Bakery, where Della bought rum cakes for special occasions and coffee ice cream. Down the street was Phil Manno's butcher shop, where DeCicco worked during high school and summers during his college years.

"I loved making Italian cut veal cutlets for my customers," he said. "Just trying to get them so thin."

He had learned a thing or two about perfection from his father, who wasn't traditionally educated but was whip smart.

"People at Martin Dennis would call my father when something wasn't working," DeCicco said. "They wouldn't call an engineer; they'd go out and get him from the crane and he'd take the whole motor apart and, with parts scattered all over a large room, he'd make the necessary repairs and get it back working again."

DeCicco often traversed the neighborhood with his mother, especially once he started attending Central High School, which was on the way to the coat factory where she worked. Each morning Della walked the two miles, past Central, to High Street and Central Avenue. For four of those years, at least, she had company along the way.

"I went to school every morning with my mother," DeCicco said.

So it only made sense that she would have something to say about where he was going next.

CHAPTER FIVE

A Dutiful Student

"If he was anywhere near the Basilica at Notre Dame, he went to the Grotto to light a candle. He was one of the most devoted Catholics I've known."

— Linda DeCicco, *Eldest daughter of Mike and Polly DeCicco*

THE FIRST FENCING FOIL DeCicco picked up was lighter than he expected.

During the swashbuckling battles he watched from a movie theater seat sandwiched between his parents, the swords always seemed to have a certain heft to them. In his hand at Salle Santelli, it felt more like an extension of his own arm.

A few guys in the neighborhood fenced, another cultural holdover from the old country. Fencing had long been a staple in Europe, particularly France, but many Italians shared the same passion and romance for the sport. For DeCicco it was perhaps a combination of that cultural pull, a love for the swashbuckling movie idols that danced across the silver screen during Saturday matinees with his father, and a bit of boyhood curiosity that first led him to hold the weapon that would become such an important part of his future.

Giorgio Santelli was already fencing royalty when DeCicco met him in 1938 at his Salle Santelli fencing club in New York

City. Giorgio was the son of Italo Santelli, the Italian fencing master who revolutionized sabre technique, but it was Giorgio Santelli who perfected it. He led the Italians to a gold medal in team sabre at the 1920 Olympic Games. He also won the Austrian, Hungarian, and Italian sabre championships, and the Austrian and Hungarian foil championships before immigrating to the U.S. in 1924.

He initially taught at the New York Athletic Club, before founding a club of his own where he trained generations of fencers. Santelli, who was the U.S. Olympic Coach in 1928, 1932, 1936, 1948, and 1952, tirelessly promoted all aspects of fencing. He established his own fencing equipment company, taught fight choreography for Broadway productions of "Hamlet," "Peter Pan," and more. He also provided free instruction to high school fencers in the region. If you wanted to learn how to fence, and lived anywhere near the city, Santelli was the one you wanted to do the teaching.

The actual motivation that put DeCicco at Salle Santelli with foil in hand for the very first time, long ago faded from his memory. But DeCicco did remember how the weapon felt in his hand, how his fingers curled around the leather hilt and his knuckles pressed against the guard. He remembered the sound of steel hitting steel and the give and take of the blade as he drove it into an opponent.

DeCicco was an attentive and dutiful student. He'd practice at home with a broom handle until he cracked the plaster on the wall, and fenced all four years for the Central High

School team. Fencing was a welcome diversion at a time when the country was preoccupied by more pressing matters.

It was during DeCicco's freshman year, just before Christmas break, that America went to war. World War II consumed American life, but particularly strained the Italian-American community. When Italy declared war on the United States in 1941 as a member of the Axis powers, many Italian Americans were only a generation removed from the home country, including the DeCiccos. Familial ties were strong and many Italian Americans wrote letters or sent money to relatives in Italy.

So it was almost understandable that the war would also bring up concerns about loyalty to their adopted home. Hundreds of Italians viewed as a potential threat to the country were interned in detention camps, some for up to two years. As many as 600,000 others, who had not become citizens, were required to carry cards identifying them as a "resident alien," and a number of Italian-language newspapers were forced to close because of past support of Fascist dictator Benito Mussolini. Most of the concerns over loyalty were quelled by the more than half a million Italian Americans who served in the various branches of the U.S. military during the war.

As DeCicco approached graduation in 1945, he knew he might also be bound for U.S. military service. Fortunately the war was nearing its end. Italian partisans killed Mussolini on April 28, and two days later Adolf Hitler committed suicide. Although Japan would fight on until August, DeCicco tried to stay focused on his college plans.

Della had been so concerned that her son would be sent to war that she made him promise to choose the first school that accepted him. DeCicco, like his father, enjoyed the mechanics of how things worked, and planned to study engineering. Although there were no college deferments during World War II, some professions—doctors, firemen, farmers, and engineers —were thought to be too valuable to the homefront to send overseas. Della knew that, too, and both she and Nick encouraged their only son to choose a path that would keep him off the front lines. Nick even asked the engineers he worked with at Martin Dennis to recommend some schools.

"One of them went to MIT (Massachusetts Institute of Technology), one went to Georgia Tech and one went to RIT (Rensselaer Institute of Technology in Troy, N.Y.), so that's where I applied," DeCicco said.

He was accepted to all three schools, but Georgia Tech's acceptance letter was the first to arrive at the Ridge Street mailbox. DeCicco kept his word, and made plans to head to Georgia.

The day of his senior prom, he was standing in his underwear ironing a pair of brown pants to wear to the dance when there was a knock at the door. It was Nick Comissa, Della's godson. The Comissas may not have found gold on the streets of America, but they were a neighborhood success story nonetheless. They started with a livery stable, which grew into an ice delivery business using their own trucks. It was a lucrative venture that allowed them to send three sons—Sal, Vince and Nick—to get a good Catholic education at Notre Dame.

As Nick Comissa entered the DeCiccos' Ridge Street residence, Della disappeared into the kitchen to get some cookies and coffee. Comissa took one look at a pants-less DeCicco and said, "Mike, what are you doing?"

"I'm getting ready for my prom," DeCicco said with the iron still in his hand.

"Prom? Are you graduating this year?" Comissa asked without really waiting for the answer. "Do you know where you're going to college?"

"Georgia Tech," DeCicco said.

"And I was proud as hell, too," he described the moment some years later.

DeCicco went on to tell Comissa that he had been accepted to all three schools and the deal he made with his mother. Della returned with refreshments just in time to hear Comissa's reaction.

"Georgia Tech?" he said. "That's the land of the Ku Klux Klan. You're going to have to take a cab to go to Mass. I bet there's not a Catholic church within 10 miles of campus."

It was that last sentence that caught Della's attention. While DeCicco was standing there with his pants down, Comissa and his mother were about to decide his future.

The DeCiccos were a devout family.

Della's father, Guiseppe DeVincenzo, had been an assistant to the local parish priest back in Pescopagano, Italy, and was able to say the entire Mass in Latin. Since coming to America, he often did so in front of an altar in his bedroom with a young DeCicco serving as his altar boy saying all the Latin responses.

Faith was also important to Nick DeCicco, who read the Bible every day after an incident on the job.

A co-worker at Martin Dennis, who spent his breaks reading scripture, told Nick that he should read from it, too. Nick wasn't easily convinced. One day, the man handed him a Bible, and Nick stuck the small Gideon into his pocket. Later that day, from the cab of the crane, Nick leaned over and the Bible fell out. He watched as it descended through the black, greasy gears.

"I guess that's the end of that," he thought.

At the end of his shift, he decided to take a look to see if it could be salvaged. Laying on the ground, to his surprise, was that same Bible without a speck of grease or dirt on it.

At that moment, Nick would tell his family later, "I decided maybe I should read it," which he did the rest of his life.

The notion that their son would not have access to church because of the Ku Klux Klan—or so Comissa had them believing—would not, could not do. So, Della asked for her godson's advice.

"He should go to Notre Dame," Comissa said. "At least he'll get a good Catholic education."

By the time Comissa had finished his coffee, Georgia Tech was out and Notre Dame was in. Della had instructed her godson to get DeCicco admitted to the University, and he promised to call Rev. Thomas Brennan at Notre Dame, to see what he could do.

"I didn't even know where the hell Notre Dame was," DeCicco said. "My mother decided where I was going. In those days, your mother said where you were going and you went."

Upon hearing from Comissa that DeCicco had been accepted to MIT, Georgia Tech and Rensselaer, Brennan accepted him on the spot.

"He said, 'If he's admitted to those three schools then he's admitted to Notre Dame.' That was it," DeCicco said. "I never even wrote an application."

On the Fourth of July, 1945, DeCicco boarded a train called "The Peacemaker" bound for Indiana. Registration was the following day in the Main Building.

The academic calendar was divided into three semesters then, and the first was the toughest for DeCicco. He missed Wednesdays at the Colonial Theater and the coffee ice cream from Ferraro's Bakery. He missed Phil Manno's butcher shop just down the street, and the sing-songy cadence of Italian being spoken in the neighborhood. Most of all, he missed his parents.

The homesickness was hard enough, but the Indiana ragweed that wreaked havoc on his hay fever added to his misery. On a long October weekend between semesters, DeCicco packed his footlocker for home with no intention of returning to campus.

When he arrived at Grand Central Terminal in New York City, Della was there to greet him. DeCicco was carrying a bag in his hands and also had a luggage ticket for his footlocker. He hadn't even made it down the ramp before she asked, "Where are you going? You're only coming home for the weekend."

DeCicco didn't lie often, and certainly not to his mother, but he wasn't quite ready to tell her the truth.

"Well," he said. "I'll leave some things home for the winter."

Della wasn't fooled. She asked to see DeCicco's return ticket. He didn't have one.

What happened next was an example of the kind of tough love DeCicco would later dole out to other young men and women struggling, like he was, to find their place at Notre Dame.

Snatching the red-cap luggage ticket from DeCicco's hand, Della dragged him by the arm to the nearest window to purchase a return ticket for her son.

"She also sent my luggage to South Bend," DeCicco said. "All the way home she's telling me, 'You're going back to finish what you started.'"

The phrase echoed in his head long after that moment at the train station, and would prove to be a mantra that would guide him for years to come.

CHAPTER SIX

Family Ties

"You want to know the best thing about Mike DeCicco? That was his wife, Polly."
— Lou Holtz, Notre Dame football coach, 1986-96

LIFE BECAME A LITTLE EASIER on the Notre Dame campus when DeCicco met Rocco Romeo, his roommate in both Zahm and Alumni halls.

Rocco was from the tiny mining town of War, West Virginia, with a population of 1,277. The official story of how the town adopted its name rests with War Creek, whose confluence with Dry Fork is located within the city limits. Town legend, however, traces the name back to 1788 where a bloody battle with the local Native American tribe took place on the land near the creek's source.

Unlike DeCicco, who was an only child, Rocco was one of five children, and the perfect person to help him acclimate to the shared living quarters of dorm life. Rocco's family lived in a house above the Romeo Grocery Store, which they ran for generations. The family shared the living quarters with Rocco's aunt, uncle and five cousins as well. Growing up, every one of the children from both families did their part to keep the business going—from stocking shelves to sweeping floors. DeCicco could relate to Rocco's familial obligations and his long list of chores to do his part in keeping the store afloat. The two also bonded over their parents' shared desire to give their children a better life than their own.

As beautiful as the Blue Ridge Mountains were, the Romeos' goal was to send each one of those children from both families far from West Virginia's hills and valleys and into a more promising life. That's why Rocco landed at Notre Dame, and it's why his younger sister, Pauline "Polly" Romeo would follow him to South Bend to attend nearby Saint Mary's College.

Polly, who was born May 22, 1929, was the youngest of the five Romeo children. She played clarinet in the Big Creek High School band, and starred as Snow White in the school play. Polly too was homesick that first year in South Bend, but she enjoyed the escapades with the girls who lived with her in her dorm. It also helped that her big brother was near.

When Polly came to Saint Mary's it was only a matter of time before Rocco introduced her to friend and roommate Mike DeCicco. Much like his parents, Nick and Della, DeCicco's first encounter with Polly happened because of family ties. What this New Jersey boy lacked, however, was the poker face his mother showed when she first saw Nick in that red sweater. It was clear to everyone, as soon as DeCicco set eyes on Polly, that he was smitten.

The introduction didn't go as smoothly as DeCicco thought it might, and he paid for it.

Polly mistook his big personality for arrogance—just another hotshot from a big city, she thought. She would prove to be a tough catch, but it only made DeCicco like her more. He sent her a Vic Damone album to win her favor, but Polly returned it, "to teach me a lesson in courtesy," DeCicco said later.

Eventually his persistence paid off, and once Polly gave DeCicco a chance, she too became smitten with a man, she discovered, that had a gentleness and kindness lying just underneath that rough exterior.

"My Dad loved her spunk," their eldest daughter, Linda DeCicco said. "He loved that about her. She didn't take his crap. She just didn't fall for it."

As their relationship bloomed, so did DeCicco. He still missed his parents, Wednesdays at the Colonial Theater and Ferraro's Bakery, but it would no longer hinder him from embracing all campus life had to offer. He and Polly went to movies and dances; attended football games and spent time just talking with friends. Then, in 1947, DeCicco learned that Notre Dame was about to resume fencing competition after a three-year hiatus due to the war. Fencing, he thought, was a piece of his New Jersey childhood that he could bring to Indiana.

"I didn't even know they had fencing at Notre Dame," DeCicco said.

Pedro DeLandero, a Spanish teacher, had started fencing as a club sport at Notre Dame in 1934. He led the Irish fencers to perfect records in both the 1935 and '36 seasons, the year it was elevated to a varsity sport. After 7-2 finishes in 1938 and '39, DeLandero, however, left the University to return to Mexico. Since he also had been Notre Dame's tennis coach from 1935-39, both jobs were vacant.

Walter Langford, who also taught Spanish at Notre Dame, took control of both the fencing and tennis programs in 1940. He knew more about tennis than fencing but still coached the Irish fencing team to a 19-13 record in three seasons until the program was suspended after the 1943 season. Scrap metal was needed during the war effort, which created a lack of weapons for the team to continue on.

When the weapons became available again and fencing resumed in 1947, Langford handed head coaching duties over to Herb Melton, a Paducah, Kentucky, native who competed in sabre under him, reaching the 1941 NCAA Championships.

Melton felt fortunate to have DeCicco—someone who had fenced before—on the squad and allowed him to compete in all three weapons—foil, sabre and epee. DeCicco was the last Notre Dame fencer to do so, compiling a 63-20 career record. But it was his 29-1 record in foil as a junior that earned him a spot in the 1948 National Championships at the United States Naval Academy in Annapolis, Maryland.

DeCicco represented Notre Dame in foil along with Bob Schlosser, in sabre, and Ralph Dixon, in epee. The three earned 21 points in the tournament, enough for a 12th-place finish, led by DeCicco's 9-5 performance.

It would be among the highlights of his career and the only time DeCicco would reach the tournament as an athlete. He finished with a career regular season foil record of 45-4, which still ranks fourth on Notre Dame's all-time list for career foil winning percentage.

While fencing may have been DeCicco's great passion, Polly was his great love. After earning his bachelor's degree in mechanical engineering in 1949, and adding a master's degree in the field a year later, he drove all the way to War, West Virginia, to ask her to marry him.

They planned to wed in New Jersey, where they would live the first years of their marriage. DeCicco had been offered an engineering job with Nash-Kelvinator Corporation on Springfield Avenue back in Newark.

Polly spent much of the year in Washington, D.C., working and planning the wedding while living with her sister, Rose. By 1952, their parents would move to nearby Silver Spring, Maryland, completing the Romeo family exodus from War, West Virginia.

Mike and Polly married on Dec. 30, 1950, at St. Lucy's Church, and the newlyweds moved into the second-floor apartment of the Ridge Street family home. Nick and Della moved upstairs to the third floor, while DeCicco's cousin, Toni, her husband and child, lived on the first floor below.

Growing up in a house with 10 children, Polly had been used to the hustle and bustle that came with it. The apartment was quiet. Although the first of the five DeCicco children, Linda and then Michele, were born there, Polly was still left alone when DeCicco and his parents went off to work each day. She missed her family, and Indiana, but she would make do.

"She's a very practical-minded person, my mother," Linda DeCicco said. "They always had an honest relationship, which was such an example for the rest of us."

In the summer of 1954, when it came time for a vacation, Mike and Polly headed to Chicago. DeCicco made sure to leave enough time for the couple to take a quick side trip on the South Shore Line from the city back to South Bend.

While Polly was visiting friends from Saint Mary's, De-Cicco went to see Karl E. Schoenherr, the dean of the College of Engineering, who also had been his graduate advisor. Schoenherr, a native of Germany, came to Notre Dame in 1945 after a 23-year career as a naval architect and marine engineer in the service of the U.S. Navy. He had been awarded the Distinguished Service Medal for his work during World War II.

DeCicco caught Schoenherr right as he was leaving for lunch.

"Mike, what have you been up to?" Schoenherr asked.

DeCicco had been working in thermodynamics, particularly contracts for air conditioning and heat transfer for Nash-Kelvinator.

"At that time, air conditioning was limited to maybe some theaters," DeCicco said.

"You know, we don't teach that course here," Schoenherr

replied. "How would you like to set up the course and set up a laboratory to cover the field?"

Schoenherr had been growing the engineering program at Notre Dame and saw an opportunity by hiring DeCicco. He would be able to provide DeCicco with a fellowship so he could earn his doctorate degree while teaching the course and creating the lab. The offer was tempting, but DeCicco was making a good salary at Nash-Kelvinator, who in 1952 introduced the Kelvinator Food-A-Rama Side-by-Side Refrigerator, one of the earliest modern side-by-side frost-free refrigerators.

"I was making $10,000 a year, plus $85 a month for a car allowance," DeCicco said. "To me that was a lot of money."

The DeCiccos also were building their own home in Scotch Plains, New Jersey. Picking up to move back to Indiana with two small children just didn't seem plausible, but by the time the DeCiccos got home from their vacation, a contract from Schoenherr was waiting for them.

"It was for $5,000 a year," DeCicco said.

Teaching positions at that time were on an eight-month contract, so to help sweeten the deal Schoenherr also promised DeCicco that he could secure him a summer job working in the research laboratory at Bendix Corporation, which designed, tested, and manufactured hydraulic components and systems mostly for the military. That would secure him another $1,000, but still $4,000 less than he was currently making.

"They both loved it here," Linda DeCicco said. "They loved the atmosphere. They loved Notre Dame. My mom wanted them to come back. They felt that Indiana was a way better place to raise children than the streets of Newark."

By Thanksgiving of 1954, the DeCiccos were supposed to be moving into their new Scotch Plains home. They never did.

"There's a time in our life, and I think other people who have gone here have felt it, too, where we feel a need to do something for Our Lady, Notre Dame, the way she did for us," DeCicco said. "I thought, well, maybe this is something I can do for her."

CHAPTER SEVEN

Coach DeCicco

"Mike DeCicco, with considerable fencing experience, especially in sabre, made a major difference to our capability, which had been rather inferior to the East Coast teams."

— *Pierre du Vair, Notre Dame fencer, 1953-57*

IT WASN'T LONG after DeCicco's return to campus, that the news found its way to Walter Langford.

Langford, who had kept the fencing program alive in the early days of World War II, had once again assumed the role of head coach in 1951.

Herb Melton, who fenced under Langford in his first tenure as head coach from 1940-43, had been picked to succeed him after the program resumed in 1947. DeCicco had been the team's star during Melton's tenure, competing in all three weapons, and compiling a 63-20 career record, which included that regular season foil mark of 45-4.

Melton's best season as Notre Dame's coach also happened to be his last. In 1950, his Irish team went undefeated at 9-0 on the way to a sixth-place finish in the NCAA tournament with foilist Nick Scalera and epeeist Ralph Dixon becoming Notre Dame's first All-Americans. At season's end, however,

Melton decided to leave Notre Dame to practice law in his hometown of Paducah, Kentucky, and Langford was again asked to take over the program.

Langford, who had also coached the Irish tennis team since 1940, leading them to the 1944 national intercollegiate championship, helped keep the fencing program alive once again. But in his second stint, his program grew beyond mere survival. It thrived, finishing in the Top 10 of the NCAAs eight times over the next 10 years with six of his fencers earning All-America honors.

Adding DeCicco as an assistant coach would be a key element of that success.

In 1954, as soon as Langford heard that DeCicco was back on campus, he sought him out. Langford had watched him fence through the Melton years and wanted DeCicco to help groom the current crop of fencers.

Although Langford was more comfortable on a tennis court than a fencing strip, he felt a commitment to the program because of his promise to Pedro DeLandero, his friend and colleague in language arts, who started Irish fencing. Langford told him he would keep fencing going at Notre Dame when DeLandero left for Mexico in 1939. Knowing that DeLandero died in Mexico City just four years later at age 55, only made Langford more aware of that promise.

A native of McAllen, Texas, Langford graduated from Notre Dame in 1930, and began teaching at the University a year later, specializing in Spanish and Portuguese instruction and Mexican literature. By 1946 he was chair of the modern languages department.

"He had never fenced himself," DeCicco said. "He was more into tennis, but he wanted to keep the fencing program alive. He once told me: 'The success of any team deals more with the assistant coaches than any head coach.' And I believed that."

Although he came back to Notre Dame to teach, DeCicco couldn't refuse Langford. He respected the man too much for saving fencing at Notre Dame. So he agreed to be his assistant coach for the 1955 season. While DeCicco was grooming new fencers, Langford, meanwhile, saw the potential to groom DeCicco to be his eventual replacement.

"Walter Langford was like a patron saint for my father," Linda DeCicco said. "He saved fencing, and my dad, I think, wanted to somehow repay him for that."

The combination of DeCicco and Langford had an almost immediate impact on the Irish. Don Tadrowski became Notre Dame's first individual champion, winning the 1955 epee title. Langford also coached the Irish to a perfect 16-0 record in 1958. Then, after the 1961 season, Langford told DeCicco he would need to guide the team from there.

Langford's service to the University took a very different turn.

Shortly after his inauguration as U.S. President in 1961, John F. Kennedy established the Peace Corps to serve underdeveloped countries in education, health care, recreation, and agriculture. Hesburgh became involved, establishing an eight-week training program at Notre Dame, which was the first of its kind sponsored by a university.

Rural Chile would be the destination for the first group of 42 Peace Corps volunteers, and Langford would be their field director for the next two years.

That left a vacancy in the coaching ranks; a vacancy DeCicco would fill as the fourth head coach in the 30-year history of the fencing program.

CHAPTER EIGHT

You Look Like a Fencer!

"He made you feel like you were a long time member of the fencing family even though you had just walked off the basketball floor."

— Jeff Pero, Notre Dame fencer, 1965-68

Langford wasn't the only loss heading into that 1961-'62 season.

DeCicco inherited just four monogram winners his first year at the helm, and the roster was peppered with fencers with little, or in some cases, no experience. The results reflected that as the Irish finished the season 7-8. It was only the third losing season in the history of the program, but it would be the only losing season in DeCicco's 34-year career.

Building on Langford's advice, and with no budget to speak of, DeCicco put in place a system to train his inexperienced squad on the strip. He would use those few with experience to teach the novice fencers the basics. Former fencers who were graduate students would become graduate assistants. But first he needed fencers.

Bulletin-board notices invited anyone and everyone to show up when fencing practice began in September. DeCicco even sent fencers into the dorms to find athletes to replenish the ranks. He knew if he had athletes, he could turn them into fencers, and he did.

"In those days there was no scholarship money," said Jeff Pero, who fenced under DeCicco from 1965-68. "There was no funding for recruiting so coach just looked for athletes. It was a varsity sport, you could get a varsity letter and it had the best winning percentage of any team on campus. He used all of that to entice people to give it a try."

Pero was one of those unlikely recruits.

As a freshman from Syracuse, New York, Pero thought, rather naively by his own admission, that he would be able to make the Notre Dame basketball team as a walk-on player. He, and a host of other former prep stars who didn't get scholarships, hit the Irish hardwood, and he, like everybody else who tried out, didn't make the cut.

"I was walking despondently off the basketball court in the old Field House heading to the exits when I heard this metal clanking sound coming from this sort of dingy room," Pero said. "I was just curious to see what was making that strange noise so I stuck my head in, looked in, and was grabbed immediately by Coach DeCicco."

Pero had stumbled upon the fencing room, and DeCicco, who noticed his sweaty basketball clothes, didn't miss a beat before selling Pero on the virtues of the sport.

"I told him my tale of woe, and he said I didn't want to play basketball anyway, that I looked like a fencer," Pero said. "He told me the basketball team's loss was the fencing team's gain. I had never even seen a fencing blade before and had no idea what a fencer did, but somehow Coach DeCicco convinced me that I ought to join the fencing team."

DeCicco's quick-witted salesman's pitch worked on Pero, and many, many others just like him. Once DeCicco had them in the room, he concentrated on the basics. He paired novice fencers with the most experienced members of the team to hasten the learning curve under his watchful eye. They trained in the repetitive movements of the sport until those movements became ingrained into their muscle memory. One of the most effective things about the regimen is that the newbies could actually see themselves becoming their more experienced teammates in a couple of years.

"When you went into the fencing room, you're thinking 'I'm in way over my head and these guys know what they're doing and I don't,'" Pero said. "But you were immediately surrounded by guys who could tell you that two years ago they were in the exact position you were in, and they were there to help you learn. It made you feel immediately like you were part of a family. You felt like you could be successful because they were successful."

The formula worked almost immediately. In DeCicco's second season, with experience in all three weapons and a roster full of eager newcomers, the Irish finished 14-2 and 10th in the NCAA tournament. In his third and fourth seasons, the Irish went 30-4 with Bill Ferrence earning All-America status in the foil by placing fourth and sixth, respectively. By the end of the 1965-66 season the Irish were 17-4 with John Bishko placing sixth in the foil in the NCAAs and DeCicco earning his first coach of the year award.

The true impact DeCicco had on those fencing teams, however, doesn't show in the records, as Pero can attest.

During the 1966-67 season, after extending their unbeaten streak to 12-0, Notre Dame faced a tough Wisconsin team. Pero, whose weapon was the epee, was not one of the top three fencers scheduled to compete that day.

"We were up a couple of bouts when the top fencer in my weapon went to coach and said, 'I've lost twice today, it's my third bout coming up, I'm going to be fencing the best fencer on the Wisconsin team and I really don't think I have it,'" Pero said. "So coach came to me."

There were three more bouts in the match and the Irish only had to win one of those to keep the unbeaten streak intact, so DeCicco figured he could put Pero in because it would be good experience for him to go up against one of the top collegiate fencers in the country. Surely, Notre Dame would win one of the other two bouts to secure the victory.

"Shortly after I started the bout the other two fencers got thrashed by Wisconsin," Pero said. "The match was now tied and the critical bout to win the match and preserve our unbeaten season was between me and a guy who almost won the national championship the year before."

DeCicco saw the panic in Pero's face and called a timeout. He walked to the young fencer standing on the strip, reached up and put his hands on Pero's shoulders.

"Jeff," he said calmly, "I know you are probably intimidated by this guy. I know you may think you can't beat him, but I know you, and I know you can. I just want you to leave the fencing strip at the end of the day knowing you did your best. If you lose and you did your best, I will be very proud of you."

Pero did his best. He won the bout and, consequently, the match, 15-12, and was carried off the floor on the shoulders of his teammates. The Irish ultimately finished the season 18-0, and after a 20-1 record the following year, Pero ended his fencing career with a ninth-place finish in the NCAA Championship for third-team All-America honors.

"Somehow he convinced me that I could do what I thought I couldn't," Pero said. "I went from a guy who had never fenced before as a freshman to an All-American as a senior. That is something I never could have contemplated. It was all because of the system that made you a part of this team. It was the chemistry in the fencing room that enabled a bunch of guys who were not stars to be able to compete at the very highest level. And all of that was because of Coach DeCicco."

CHAPTER NINE

All-Time Winningest Coach

"In the gym it didn't take long to realize what everybody thought of Coach DeCicco. They respected him and loved him and adored him."
— Mike Sullivan, Notre Dame fencer, 1976-79

ALTHOUGH NOTRE DAME'S reputation in the collegiate fencing community was growing, its Midwest location and lack of scholarships was still a tough sell. Youth fencing in America was largely limited to the East Coast, and East Coast colleges, including perennial power New York University, which often had their pick of the best fencers during recruiting season.

DeCicco understood that. When he first left New Jersey for Indiana all those years ago he expected to find the Notre Dame campus planted between cornfields. To truly grow the fencing program DeCicco needed to convince at least a handful of top recruits to come to Notre Dame.

"Fencing is a rather small community and Coach DeCicco had standing in that community," said Mike Sullivan, who fenced under DeCicco from 1976-79. "He had become a figure in United States fencing and used that to bring the Junior World Fencing Championships here."

DeCicco helped organize three Junior World Fencing Championships on the Notre Dame campus in 1971, 1979 and 1988, and another in 2000 at the Century Center in South Bend. It was through such events that DeCicco met Joe Pechinsky.

Pechinsky and his Tanner City Fencing Club was as revered in Peabody, Massachusetts, as Giorgio Santelli's Salle Santelli fencing club had been in New York City during DeCicco's childhood. Pechinsky, who survived the bombing of Pearl Harbor while stationed in Hawaii in the U.S. Army in 1941, first started coaching in the 1960s out of the Salem, Massachusetts YMCA. He was a firefighter who sometimes gave fencing students lessons between the fire trucks inside Station 7 while waiting for the next alarm.

By the 1970s, the Y could no longer hold his students so he started Tanner City, which became a place where veteran fencers were expected to give lessons to newcomers, and Pechinsky often coached without compensation.

Sullivan, who grew up in Peabody, Massachusetts, started fencing under Pechinsky's tutelage when he was 8 years old.

"At that age I had a lot of natural aggressive tendencies apparently," Sullivan said. "Joe learned how to teach fencing but never learned how to fence."

Sullivan, who was one of the top foil fencers in the country, started fencing sabre in competition and was the Junior National Champion when he was 17 and 18 years old.

"I was a hot recruit, such as it is in the fencing world,"

Sullivan said. "North Carolina and North Carolina State of-fered some scholarship money but they didn't have very strong programs. Scholarships in those days were few and far between, but financial aid was a possibility for me because my family didn't have any money."

DeCicco was also pursuing Sullivan to come to Notre Dame, and hopped on a plane for Boston to try to close the deal.

"He didn't have (a full-ride scholarship) to give, but he put together a financial-aid package that included Pell grants that I was just eligible for and a small student loan and a scholarship from a Boston alumni group," Sullivan said. "He took us to this fabulous restaurant, which was the kind of place my family didn't go, and did the full Mike DeCicco show."

A few months later Sullivan walked onto the Notre Dame campus having never seen the place and straight into DeCicco's office with one suitcase and his fencing bag.

Irish fencing returned to the national conversation a year before Sullivan arrived by claiming third at the 1975 NCAAs led by All-Americans Tim Glass (epee), Mike McCahey (foil) and Sam DiFiglio (sabre). Although Sullivan was a natural foil fencer, DeCicco already had a competition brewing between McCahey and fellow sophomore Pat Gerard at the weapon. He needed a sabreist to follow DiFiglio, and Sullivan was it. Behind Sullivan, who placed third, and Glass, who was fourth, the third-place Irish were once again in contention for the 1976 NCAAs.

It all clicked in 1977. The Irish fencers went 23-0 in dual meets heading into the NCAA tournament, which was held at the Joyce Center on the Notre Dame campus. The Irish finished the round-robin tied with NYU for first place at 114 points. Three previous ties had led to co-champs but a new NCAA format called for a tiebreaking fence-off to declare a winner.

Sabre was contested first. Miklos Benedek took a 3-2 lead before Sullivan, the individual sabre champion, rallied to win 5-3. Gerard was the individual foil champion, but he and Tom Valjasic had split two earlier bouts 5-4. In the tiebreaker, Gerard jumped ahead 3-0, closing out the tiebreaker and the title in a 5-0 bout. Gerard's win meant Glass, who finished fourth individually, didn't have to compete in the fence-off against epee champion Hans Wieselgren as the Irish stormed the floor.

"After he mopped up Tom Valjasic I just picked up Gerard and everyone came charging in," Sullivan said.

The day concluded with DeCicco being named coach of the year, an honor he also received in 1966, '75 and '92.

The Irish repeated as national champions in 1978 led by back-to-back sabre champ Mike Sullivan, foil runner-up Pat Gerard, and epee champ Bjorn Vaggo. The team was one of the most dominant in NCAA history as the Irish ran away from the field at Wisconsin-Parkside. The power trio was 102-5 in the regular season, including 41-0 from Sullivan.

Notre Dame—led by NCAA foil champ Andy Bonk—added a runner-up finish in 1979, and its six-year, 122-match winning streak finally ended in 1980.

Getting Mike Sullivan certainly helped Notre Dame fencing in the short term, but it also opened up a pipeline of fencing talent between Pechinsky's Tanner City Fencing Club and DeCicco's Irish.

"There had to be more than a dozen of us that went from Pechinsky to DeCicco," Sullivan said.

The first woman in that group was Molly Sullivan Sliney.

The Irish added women's fencing in 1977, but it hadn't had the same level of success as the men's team. DeCicco had laid the foundation, but mostly relied on his men's team and graduate assistants to help coach the women's squad. After the 1984-85 season, he came up with a plan to change that of course, and once again it began by getting on a plane to Boston.

Molly Sullivan Sliney started fencing under Pechinsky when she was 10, and by 13 she had made her first world team. She was being heavily recruited by several colleges with strong women's fencing programs, making Notre Dame a long shot at best when DeCicco came calling.

"They had no women's program that had been successful, it was located in the Midwest, which made traveling to international competitions difficult, and they had no coach,"

Sullivan Sliney said. "There was nothing that attracted me to Notre Dame except for it being a fantastic school—until I met Coach DeCicco."

When DeCicco met Sullivan Sliney and her parents for lunch, he actually had a scholarship to offer. Over the course of that luncheon he discovered that money and where to hang her fencing foil weren't the biggest obstacles facing Sullivan Sliney's college decision.

"I'm dyslexic," Sullivan Sliney said. "I was diagnosed when I was in first grade and I had someone who worked with me privately all through school. When I was looking at Notre Dame there was no program in place for kids with learning disabilities so that was another negative."

That's when DeCicco stopped his pitch, and made her a promise.

"He said to me, 'Yes, you're a great fencer, but what I can give you is a great education,'" Sullivan Sliney said. "'We will pay for your schooling, and you will be taken care of.' He was the academic advisor, and I knew that I was going to need a lot of support. He was very straightforward about what he would do for me and what he wanted me to do for them. I don't know how to explain it, but when Coach DeCicco made a promise like that, you knew he was going to follow through."

Among the promises he made Sullivan Sliney that day was to bring in a full-time women's fencing coach by her sophomore year. He tapped Yves Auriol, who at that time had already served as coach for the women's U.S. Olympic team in 1980, and '84. He also had served as coach for the U.S. at the Junior World Championships from 1976-79 and guided the U.S. at the 1977 World University Games in Bulgaria and at the 1978 World Championships in Hamburg, West Germany.

In that 1986 season, the Irish men won their third NCAA title behind foilists Yehuda Kovacs (runner-up) and Charles Higgs-Coulthard (third), epeeists Mike Gostigian (third) and Christian Scherpe (fourth), and sabreists Don Johnson (sixth) and John Edwards.

The women, meanwhile, finished second in the NCAA with Sullivan Sliney winning the foil title. She placed third in 1987, and Notre Dame's women team—behind Sullivan Sliney, Janice Hynes, Kristin Kralicek and Anne Barreda—won their first NCAA title.

A year later, Sullivan Sliney returned to Princeton's Jadwin Gym and won her second NCAA title—equaled by just four other Notre Dame student-athletes—with Barreda finishing third to match the team's finish.

"When I met Coach DeCicco, he said he wanted to build one of the best women's programs in the country," Sullivan Sliney said. "He wanted to bring me in and create a program around me. My sophomore year he said he was going to bring in Yves who was the Olympic coach, and he did all that and more."

The list of accomplishments by Notre Dame fencing teams under DeCicco is almost endless.

DeCicco's teams won almost 95 percent of their matches.

He finished with a staggering 680-45 (.938) career coaching record, which is still the winningest coaching record in Irish history. A combined team title in 1994 gave him five national championships, eight NCAA individual champs, a 122-match winning streak spanning six seasons (including four undefeated seasons), 12 undefeated and nine one-loss campaigns, almost 100 All-Americans and four national coach-of-the-year selections in a 34-year coaching career.

"I went there for four years, and the thing that never changed, that never wavered, was what he promised me at that luncheon," Sullivan Sliney said. "We both lived up to our part of the bargain. There are a lot of people you meet in life who don't always live up to what they promise you, but with him, he always did."

CHAPTER TEN

Changing Attitudes, Not Grades

"When we started having study sessions, we had a list of who needed help and we made them sign in and out. If the list came back and you weren't there, I'd haul you into the office."

— Mike DeCicco, Notre Dame academic advisor, 1964-92

IT WASN'T LONG after his meeting with Joyce about the now infamous pink slip incident that DeCicco began sending his new academic advising questionnaire to faculty members across campus.

The four questions DeCicco had scribbled on the back of an envelope—about attendance, grades, and tutoring help—were met with derision among some members of the academic community. They saw the questionnaire as a tool the University would use to coddle athletes, or worse, ask faculty members to hold them to a different standard.

Fortunately, DeCicco's reputation as a coach and as a member of the faculty himself afforded him a certain level of respect among both athletics and academics, as did his backing by Joyce and Hesburgh.

"He was a professor, and he also had the No. 2 guy at the University, in Father Ned Joyce, in full support of anything he did," Hesburgh said. "And he knew he had my full support so it was clean cut from the top to the bottom."

DeCicco asked the college deans to speak to their faculty, letting every professor know that his focus was about education, not changing grades. If student-athletes weren't going to class, or were flunking, DeCicco wanted to know it so he could help them as soon as possible.

"We just wanted to know who needed to be kicked in the tail," DeCicco said. "If they're not going to class, we want to know it. And if they're flunking, we want to know it so we might be able to help them."

That meant that DeCicco had to be on top of each student-athlete's progress on a week-to-week basis, not just after the warning signs were too great to overcome. He saw too many athletes who had a last-minute comeback mentality in the classroom, so he became a martinet when it came to demanding consistent academic success. But he also knew he could no longer do it alone.

"Everything I ended up doing was by trial and error, and the reports worked," DeCicco said. "But it wasn't a one-man job anymore. I had to ask Father Joyce to increase my budget so I could get some kids to read every one of those reports."

William Leahy, who was working on his doctorate in economics, was the first graduate student hired by DeCicco. Others would soon follow.

The deans supplied DeCicco with a list of graduate students who might make good tutors, students who could teach any subject. "That helped. That helped a lot," DeCicco said. Tutors were especially needed during freshman year. "Math was always a problem. The sciences were always a problem."

For example, DeCicco recalled former student Willie Fry, whose high school didn't offer science as a class. Fry was a "very, very good student," DeCicco said. "He just needed some help."

The coaches, athletes and faculty all soon discovered that DeCicco's help meant more work, not less.

"We did everything we could to help them," Hesburgh said. "If they needed a tutor, we got them a tutor, but we didn't fudge anything. They had to take their own exams and write their own papers. It became pretty obvious there weren't going to be any deals under the table here."

Academic advising expanded from a fledgling program for football players, to an office that encompassed all student-athletes on campus. DeCicco created mandatory study sessions, and worked with the University to add a 10-day orientation program that taught time management and proper ways to study, as well as summer school classes in subjects that demanded too much time or conflicted with practices during the regular school year.

"Organic chemistry was at 3 in the afternoon and then there was a laboratory until 5 so they'd miss two days of class to go to practice," DeCicco said. "We got them to offer organic chemistry in the summer as well, so that every student-athlete who wanted to go into medicine had to go to summer school.

Then the business students wanted statistics in the summer to get that out of the way. Every major had a course or two they would love to have available during the summer."

While much of the university community saw what DeCicco was trying to accomplish, some members of the faculty resisted the change. There were those who refused to fill out his questionnaire, and DeCicco occasionally had to fight old stereotypes about his "dumb jocks" on multiple fronts.

One of those incidents involved basketball star Adrian Dantley who, along with Ray Martin, came into DeCicco's office visibly nervous after a teacher claimed they had cheated on their math final.

DeCicco looked at Dantley and asked, "Did you?"

"Of course not," Dantley replied. "We did exactly what you told us."

To prevent such accusations, DeCicco told athletes not to sit together in class.

"One guy sat in the front of the class and one guy sat in the back just so they weren't even close," DeCicco said. "Most of our athletes did that. So I said to Adrian, 'Did the teacher know that?'"

"Yeah," Dantley replied. "And they still said we cheated."

DeCicco attended the academic hearing knowing something other than the math test didn't add up.

During the hearing, Dantley's math teacher told the disciplinary board that even though Dantley and Martin were sitting apart, he knew they cheated, DeCicco recalled. When the board asked how he could tell, the teacher said that they solved a problem the same way, and that they were the only two to do so.

DeCicco left the room and found the graduate student who had been tutoring them at math. He explained what was happening, and brought him into the hearing.

"I have the tutor that Adrian and Martin studied with," DeCicco told the board. "I'd like you to ask him how to solve the problem."

The tutor used the same method that Dantley and Martin had. When he was finished he said, "I told them that you can solve it this way, and it would be a lot easier."

The board members accepted the tutor's explanation, "as they should have," DeCicco said. "Those guys did not cheat. They solved the problem like they were taught in a study session. But that professor still believed they got away with murder."

Afterward, DeCicco and the chairman of the math department spoke privately with Dantley and Martin's math teacher, and discovered why he was so adamant in his belief that the young men had cheated.

The math teacher, DeCicco recalled, was from South Africa and told them about living two or three blocks from an all-black school. Every day, those students would walk by his house, which had a large fruit tree in the front yard. One morning, all the fruit on his tree was gone.

"I know," he told DeCicco, "one of those niggers did it. None of them would admit it, but I still know they did."

DeCicco was livid.

It was hard enough getting student-athletes to see a tutor. He didn't need to combat bigoted professors as well. DeCicco pulled the math chair aside and said, "You know if I went to Father Hesburgh's office and told him what this guy just said, he'd be calling you five minutes later to have you can his ass!"

"He looked at me and said, 'Mike, don't worry. He won't be teaching here again.'"

CHAPTER ELEVEN

A Rusty Blade

"He had the respect of everybody in the athletic department and the respect of student athletes. That's what made it so successful."
— Roger Valdiserri, Notre Dame Sports Information Director, 1957-95

THERE ARE STORIES told so often, stories passed from one student class to another, that they become campus legends. Notre Dame certainly has its share of them. So it should come as little surprise that a Notre Dame man like DeCicco should be the subject of one such tale.

The story is part fable, part fact, and, depending on who is doing the telling, features DeCicco, a cowering 300-pound Notre Dame football player, and a rusty sabre that DeCicco had hanging on his office wall.

Many people will tell you that they had a teammate or knew the guy that this happened to, but the particular student-athlete or athletes in question remain a mystery.

DeCicco summoned a football player into his office on one particular day to talk about his failing academic performance, or so the story goes. The football player, not taking DeCicco too seriously, made some sort of wisecrack, and DeCicco leapt into action.

"He'd say, 'You see that sabre on the wall?'" former Notre Dame Sports Information Director Roger Valdiserri recalled. "'If I see you in here again I'll run this rusty sabre up your backside!' They knew he meant business."

The variations of the legend have DeCicco jumping onto his desk or grabbing the sabre off the wall. The threat also varies between rendering the young man unable to have children or otherwise making it difficult for the student-athlete to sit for quite some time.

"Everybody tells that story," Mike Sullivan said. "That tells me that it was quite a word of mouth thing, or that DeCicco did it with some frequency with an audience because he knows what works. He knows if he gets a football player in there and there are five others waiting to go in, they're all going to hear the same message."

Whether this incident happened or not, the truth remains that DeCicco could be an intimidating presence when pushed too far. And he had the authority to push back.

"He had a temper that the athletes saw," former Notre Dame football coach Lou Holtz said. "He was a very strong disciplinarian. He was tough. He gave them a lot of tough love, but he also really cared about them."

Linda DeCicco, who worked in her father's office filing and updating fencing lists during high school and college summers, often witnessed the spectacle.

"I remember guys coming in grumbling about him who didn't know I was his daughter," she said. "But as soon as he opened that door, they jumped to it. He had a lot of power and they knew it so they jumped through whatever hoops they had to go through to keep their eligibility. He always was able to keep their eye on the prize."

And that prize was graduation.

The graduation rates among student-athletes during DeCicco's tenure as academic advisor set a new standard. Some years it was nearly perfect, other years it dipped slightly regardless of his efforts. All told, however, the average graduation rate among student-athletes at Notre Dame under DeCicco was 98 percent.

When asked about it, DeCicco deflected most of the credit to the academic atmosphere created by Joyce and Hesburgh, and the cooperation he received from Notre Dame's coaches. But ultimately it came down to DeCicco's talent to get through to those student-athletes even if it meant an idle threat with a rusty sabre.

"He could go out to a football practice or a basketball practice and grab anyone off the field or off the court," Valdiserri said. "If they had an assignment due and didn't do it, he'd go get them. If they missed a class, he'd want to know why. They would be in that office shaking until he came in."

Former Notre Dame basketball coach Digger Phelps often gets questions about how he graduated 100 percent of his players. All of the 56 student-athletes Phelps recruited from 1971-91 graduated.

In *Tales from the Notre Dame Hardwood*, Phelps points to

DeCicco's tenacity, including pulling players out of basketball practice to settle academic issues.

"When I came in the locker room before practice and said 'DeCicco needs to see one of you,' everyone stood still," Phelps wrote. "I would pause for about a minute while the players squirmed, then I would call out the name or names."

It would have been an impossible job, DeCicco said, if the coaches weren't on board.

Luckily, when DeCicco initially got the academic advisor assignment, Ara Parseghian was Notre Dame's new football coach. Parseghian, who had come to Notre Dame following coaching stints at Miami University in Ohio and Northwestern University, had thought this was just how things were done at Notre Dame.

"I thought Mike had always been doing this," Parseghian said. "When I was at Miami of Ohio and Northwestern, we as a staff followed the players. We were the ones who did the advising and so forth. I was delighted they had a program like that. Next thing you know he's got basketball and baseball and the whole kit and caboodle. If coaches didn't listen to what he said, they were cutting off their own heads."

When it came to academic advising, DeCicco's initial partnership with Parseghian became a model for other coaches that followed, allowing the program itself to grow.

Could a program that put academic success above its on-field success be a contender when it came to wins and losses? It was a legitimate question. Parseghian's 1966 Irish team

provided the answer by winning the national championship—even with DeCicco hot on their heels.

Terry Hanratty, who would go on to win two Super Bowl
rings as Terry Bradshaw's backup with the Pittsburgh Steelers,
was Notre Dame's quarterback on that team. Although he
admits now that academics wasn't exactly his strength, Hanratty said DeCicco made it clear that even the Irish's starting
quarterback had to make the grade. That included showing up
to every class.

"He'd come into the locker room and I'd hide," Hanratty
said, laughing. "He'd yell, 'Hanratty, I know you're in here
somewhere!' You couldn't get away with anything."

While detractors said such scrutiny would only add to the
on-field pressure, Parseghian found the opposite was true.
DeCicco made sure every student-athlete knew where they
stood academically. If there was even a hint of a struggle,
DeCicco was there.

"It may not transpose into blocking and tackling and game
preparation but it does help the unity of a team knowing you're
not going to get kicked off the next day," Parseghian said. "But
the long-term gift he gave them was to make sure they graduated in whatever field they were in. Take a look at where they
are now and where they would have been if they hadn't gotten
their academic degree. He's transformed lives."

Gerry Faust, who was the Irish football coach from 1981-
85, said he was introduced to DeCicco on Day 1. In that meeting, Joyce made the pecking order abundantly clear.

"He said, 'Mike's in charge of academics, period,' " Faust recalled. "I never questioned it."

"He knew that he had my full cooperation," added Holtz, who coached the Irish from 1986-96, winning the 1988 national championship. "If a guy was missing class or in any kind of academic trouble, I wanted to know about it. They're here to get an education. If they aren't eligible, they aren't going to play one second for us."

"I just think they realized there wasn't anything I wanted them to do for my benefit," DeCicco said. "It was for the kids. It was for their benefit. Academics simply came first. For me, and my staff, well, our bowl game was a degree."

Mike DeCicco, Notre Dame Student, 1945

d

Mike DeCicco, Notre Dame Student, 1947

Mike DeCicco, Notre Dame Fencer, 1949

Mike and his parents, Nicola and Della DeCicco, on the steps
of the Notre Dame Administration Building, 1949

Pauline "Polly" Romeo with her parents and siblings in West Virginia, 1940
Front Row (l-r): Polly, Joseph (father), Rocco (brother);
Middle Row (l-r): Rose (sister), Carmella ("Nellie") (mother);
Back Row (l-r): Matthew ("Butch") (brother), Francis ("Chic") (sister)

Polly Romeo and Mike DeCicco, Sophomore Cotillion, 1948

NOTRE DAME FENCING TEAM — 1948 TEAM PICTURE
"MELTON'S MUSKETEERS II"

1st Row: P. Gross, R. Witucki, R. Schlosser, R. Bosler, J. Lubin, W. Wier, L. Burns (Captain)

2nd Row: M. DeCicco, T. Roney, J. Jansen, R. Dixon, Herb Melton (Coach), Walter Langford (faculty Advisor), Lou Peck (Ass't. Coach), C. McDonald, C. Marshall, E. Martin J. Vincent

Mike and Polly's Wedding Day, Newark, New Jersey - December 30, 1950

d

Notre Dame Fencers, 1960
Front Row (l-r): Jim Russomano, Jerry Johnson, Ted DeBaene. Back Row (l-r): Mike DeCicco, Peter Giaimo, Jim Radde, Walter Langford

d

Mike DeCicco, Head Coach — Fencing, 1962

Two head coaches at Notre Dame from Newark, New Jersey: Mike DeCicco (Fencing) and Hugh Devore (Football), 1963

(l-r) Moose Krause, Athletic Director; Ara Parseghian, Head Football Coach; and Mike DeCicco in 1966

University of Notre Dame Leaders, 1964
Executive Vice President, Father Ned Joyce, and President, Father Ted Hesburgh

Executive Vice-President   September 1, 1965   Cable Address "Dulac"

Mr. Michael A. DeCicco
Freshman Year of Studies
University of Notre Dame

Dear Mike:

I am delighted that you have decided to accept
our invitation to become the director of the tutorial
program for the Notre Dame athletes. Your position as a
respected member of the Notre Dame faculty, the counseling
experience you have gained in your work with the Office of
the Freshman Year, and your own particular interest in
Notre Dame athletes augurs well for the continued success
of this highly important program.

I have discussed our arrangements with Dean
Gay and he will reduce your teaching load for the coming
academic year to one three-hour course. You will, of
course, continue your work with Dean Burke in the Freshman
Year and the balance of your time can be given to the
tutorial program.

You will also receive an additional stipend of
$500.00 from athletic funds for your direction of the
tutorial program. By means of a copy of this letter, I am
instructing Mr. Harwood to remit this sum to you, at your
request, any time during the academic year.

With best wishes for your success, I am

Sincerely yours,

Edmund P. Joyce, csc

(Rev.) Edmund P. Joyce, C.S.C.
Executive Vice President

cc: Mr. Harwood

Father Joyce Letter to the first Director of the Tutorial Program, 1965

Mike DeCicco, Director of the Tutorial Program, 1965

Mike DeCicco, Director of Tutorial Program, 1970

Mike and Polly DeCicco with their five children, 1970
Front Row (l-r): Michael, Polly and Mike Back Row (l-r): Della, Michele, Nick and Linda

d

Alan Page, All-American, 1966

Jeff Pero, All-American, 1968

d

Adrian Dantley, All-American, 1976

Mike Sullivan, All-American, 1977

Molly Sullivan Sliney, All-American, 1987

Mike and Father Joyce, 1987

Mike and Polly, 1991

Mike and Polly with their 5 children and 14 grandchildren
(12 great-grandchildren not in this picture), 1999

Polly's induction as an honorary member of the Notre Dame Monogram Club, 1993

Polly, Father Hesburgh and Mike, 1994

Pat Holmes, Director of Academic Services for Student-Athletes since 2003

John Lium, 1967 (member of the 1966 National Championship Football Team) with his son, John Michael Lium, 2012

Ron Jeziorski, 1967 — member of the 1966 National Championship Football Team.
Ron had the vision and was the inspiration for the publication of this book,
A Notre Dame Man: The Mike DeCicco Story.

CHAPTER TWELVE

Touching Lives

"I think a lot of coaches do it for their success. They think they somehow own their athletes, but that's not what you felt with Coach DeCicco. With him there was no ownership, only strength." — Molly Sullivan Sliney, Notre Dame fencer, 1986-88

THE GRUFFNESS DECICCO showed in his office may have masked his feelings to most student-athletes at Notre Dame, but not John Lium.

Lium, an offensive lineman on the '66 national championship team, was the son of a Norwegian farm boy, but his mother was all Italian. Lium grew up in the Bronx, New York, where his mother's eight brothers and sisters all lived within a 2-mile radius.

He first met DeCicco when the mandatory study hall sessions were implemented. He and about five other football players were called into DeCicco's office and told about the new program. One of them made the mistake of asking why they had to do it.

According to Lium, DeCicco got in everyone's face, and said, "Because I'm telling you to!"

As they were leaving, Lium gave DeCicco a hug, which baffled his teammates.

"What's the matter with you?" one of them said. "That guy's yelling and screaming at us and you hug him when we leave?"

"You don't understand," Lium replied. "That guy was just showing how much he cared about us. That's Italian family tough love."

For the one-time visitors, that Italian tough love was all they saw. Those who spent more than one occasion in DeCicco's office, however, soon learned that the only thing that dwarfed his big personality was his commitment to their education.

"I know there were professors who thought he was doing a disservice to academics. I know there were probably some people who thought he was doing a disservice to athletics," Linda DeCicco said. "He was always caught in the middle."

Still, DeCicco's role as academic advisor became a crusade, his own personal investment in every individual who struggled to balance a rigorous academic and athletic schedule. The results were tangible.

"He can read people and know what's going to be good for them," Molly Sullivan Sliney said. "That's what I felt was so stunning. He told me right away, 'I don't want you rooming with other fencers.' I didn't understand at the time, but it was to give me the experience of college. He didn't want it to be all fencing. I don't know how to explain how important that was."

DeCicco also made sure Sullivan Sliney had everything she needed to cope with her severe dyslexia—even when what she needed was a place to retreat to when it all became too much.

"There was more than a couple of times that I would walk into his office and I would close the door and I would sit down and I would just start crying," Sullivan Sliney said. "He would just hear babble, babble, babble, cry, cry, cry. And he'd say that it would be all right. And I knew that just hearing him say that, that it would be all right."

Adrian Dantley, who was named the national player of the year in 1975-76 by the United States Basketball Writers Association, decided to pass up his senior season to make himself available for the NBA draft in 1976. Before he left campus, DeCicco made Dantley promise that he would return to campus to complete his degree.

After playing on the United States Olympic basketball team that won the gold medal in Montreal in 1976, and being named the NBA rookie of the year in 1977 with a 20.3 scoring average for the Buffalo Braves, Dantley did just that, completing his undergraduate studies in 1978. Dantley played 15 seasons in the NBA, and his 23,177 career points ranks 21st all-time. When Dantley was inducted into Notre Dame's Ring of Honor in 2012 during halftime of the Notre Dame-Providence game, his thoughts turned to family and DeCicco.

"The three people who got me through Notre Dame were my mother, my aunt, and Mr. DeCicco," he said to the crowd. "They were the three people who got me through academically."

For Jeff Pero, his moments with DeCicco often come flooding into his memory, including the time his interview for the Root-Tilden Scholarship at New York University's School of Law happened to coincide with a fencing tournament in Chicago.

"When it came time for the interview, DeCicco sent me in the team bus over to the federal courthouse to make sure I would get there, and when I came back to the hotel, coach was waiting for me," Pero said.

He got the scholarship, and four years ago, when Pero was back on campus he was reminded of that moment. Pero was showing his family and friends where he used to fence when he saw a light. Pero hadn't seen DeCicco in 20 years, but poked his head into the office.

"He immediately said 'Jeff Pero!' and then began beguiling my wife and my friends with stories about my fencing exploits," Pero said. "But the first thing he said was, 'You know Jeff won the Root-Tilden Scholarship.' To him, it was the most important thing he could say to them."

Alan Page, whose pink slip inspired DeCicco to create the faculty questionnaire, was playing defensive tackle with the Minnesota Vikings when he asked DeCicco if he would write a recommendation for him for law school. DeCicco beamed, but couldn't help but ask two of Page's Vikings teammates who had played for a rival school, what their offseason plans were.

"I said, 'So Alan is going to law school, what are you guys

going to do? What major did you have in school?'" DeCicco said.

"We were both in education, but we never graduated," one of them responded.

"Never graduated?" DeCicco asked. "Did you finish four years of school?"

They both said yes, but when they went to their coach to get tickets for their parents to attend graduation, they were directed to the department chairman. The chairman informed them they were both a number of courses shy of graduating.

"They said, 'What do you mean? I took every course that our coaches worked out for me. I didn't flunk anything,'" DeCicco recalled. "They had them taking offensive and defensive football classes and other courses the coaches were offering instead. I suspect there were a hell of a lot of schools that were doing that."

DeCicco did write Page a recommendation for the University of Minnesota's law school. And after a 15-year NFL tenure, he started practicing law full-time. Today he is an associate justice of the Minnesota Supreme Court and a member of both the College Football Hall of Fame and the Pro Football Hall of Fame.

"He cared about them when they were here and he cared about them when they left," Valdiserri said of DeCicco. "He was always interested in what they were doing after graduation and in promoting their chances of getting into grad school and even doctorates. I'm not sure a lot of people do that."

When Lium's son, John Michael, told his father that he wanted to study computer science at Notre Dame, the elder Lium was skeptical. He had wanted his son to follow in his footsteps, studying finance before heading to law school.

After failing to convince his son, Lium called DeCicco to seek his advice. He hoped DeCicco would somehow convince the younger Lium to come around to his father's way of thinking. DeCicco agreed to take the young student to lunch to get a sense of John Michael. It wasn't long after that lunch that DeCicco called Lium back.

"Success in life is doing what you're passionate about, and your boy is beyond passionate about this field," DeCicco said. "I will guarantee you today that he will have a job at graduation."

Lium backed off. His son graduated with a degree in computer science in 2012 and was offered a job at Notre Dame's tech hub, Innovation Park, as DeCicco had predicted.

At a celebration dinner, DeCicco talked about how John Michael Lium didn't need any academic help to do so either —unlike his father.

DeCicco looked right at Lium with a knowing grin, then turned his attention to Lium's son.

"You know, John," DeCicco said to the new graduate, "your father is living proof that good looks and intelligence skips a generation."

"All I could say," Lium recalled, "Was, you know, you son of a gun, you may be right."

For every Alan Page or Adrian Dantley, Jeff Pero or Molly Sullivan Sliney, there are thousands more just like them. Generations of students owe DeCicco and his staff for their education and careers.

They may have come to Notre Dame as athletes, but they left as graduates. They will tell you that they learned that life in sport is short, but an education is forever. They will also tell you that Mike DeCicco was the one who taught them the lessons they still carry throughout their lives.

"He loved the people in his life in a way that I've never encountered before," Pero said. "Next to my father, he is the most influential person in my entire life."

"He was Uncle Mike to me and a lot of my teammates," Lium said. "You actually felt like you were part of his family and he was a part of your family."

"If you don't have direction, what path do you think a kid is going to go down?" Parseghian said. "This university was interested in the total person and Mike DeCicco was behind that."

"In his office is where he coached me," Mike Sullivan said. "What he taught was leadership."

"He touches people in such an important time in their life," Sullivan Sliney said. "Between 18-21 you're really building who you are going to be for the rest of your life. I think a lot of people who have come to Notre Dame have been blessed to have him as one of the foundations of that."

DeCicco served in some capacity at Notre Dame for 41 years. The academic advising program that he started has since become the model for countless other schools and positioned the University as the leader in showing how athletics and academics can be mutually supportive and beneficial to student-athletes.

DeCicco often deflected such statements, underplaying his role as just another cog in a wheel propelled by Hesburgh and Joyce. But in practice, DeCicco was much more than that. He was a kindred spirit, a surrogate father, a confidante and staunch defender.

With each new year, DeCicco was reminded in the faces of incoming freshmen, that on every team there were students just like him. He saw in them the boy from Newark, New Jersey, who so many years earlier had traded the Colonial Theater and Ferraro's Bakery for the green fields and Golden Dome of the Irish campus. They came from all corners of the United States to play ball and get an education. Like him, they packed a suitcase, and headed for South Bend, Indiana, sometimes sight unseen. For many it was only through sports that such an education was possible. They were challenged physically, mentally and socially. Many were homesick. Others were overwhelmed.

DeCicco remembered how he once boarded a train for

home vowing not to return to campus, and how his mother, thankfully, sent him back, to stick it out. He remembered those times when Sullivan Sliney crumpled in his office, or Dantley sought his help in fighting a bogus cheating accusation. He lived the struggle of every one of his charges, and celebrated every victory whether it was the 1966 national football championship or the Root-Tilden Scholarship.

In academic advising circles, he's a pioneer. To the fencing community, he's simply "Coach." And at Notre Dame, he's a legend.

"I wasn't anybody," DeCicco said. "I came here because my mother told me to."

EPILOGUE

MIKE DECICCO retired as the head of academic advising in 1992, and three years later hung up his coaching duties and that rusty sabre for good.

Despite his retirement after 41 years of service, he still remained a fixture on the Notre Dame campus and kept an office on emeritus status at Father Hesburgh's request.

"What I didn't know," DeCicco said while sitting in an overstuffed chair in his home, "was emeritus meant you work for free."

The academic advising program DeCicco started five decades ago in an office carved out of a men's restroom is now known as Academic Services for Student Athletes and is located in the bottom floor of the Coleman-Morse Center on Notre Dame's quad.

Since 2003, Patrick Holmes, a 1977 Notre Dame graduate who worked under DeCicco, has been the program's director. Although the name has changed and the program has grown significantly to address the needs of nearly 800 student-athletes, Holmes and his full-time staff of eight still use many of the tools and guidelines created by DeCicco.

The office remains separated from the athletic department, and all first-semester student-athletes are required to take part in eight hours of mandatory supervised study hall a week. The office hires its own set of nearly 200 tutors a semester who are independent from other tutoring programs on campus, and largely selected based on recommendations from professors and department heads.

Holmes and his counselors still help student-athletes manage their schedules and lives, help with course selections, and track progress towards degree completion.

The staff keeps organized records of every player's academic performance and study habits, and the office space —open 7 days a week—is routinely filled with student-athletes dropping in for a tutoring session held in one of the several glass-walled rooms that line the facility.

Summer school remains a key tool. Incoming freshmen athletes are thrust into a summer bridge program. Scholarship athletes in football and men's basketball and women's basketball, along with a smattering of players from other sports, spend the summer on campus taking a handful of classes and meeting with the academic staff while they're going through preseason workouts.

The numbers offer statistical proof on just how successful the program has been.

The College Sports Information Directors of America began recognizing Academic All-American Athletes in 1952. Since that time, 222 Notre Dame student-athletes have been recognized in all sports and 56 in football. Forty-seven of those Irish football players have been named All-Americans since the academic advisory program began. Another 17 former Irish football players have received post-graduate scholarships in recognition of their academic achievements.

The NCAA's Graduation Success Rate numbers among the 120 Football Bowl Subdivision schools consistently rank Notre Dame at No. 1. The October 2012 GSR figures for football listed Notre Dame and Northwestern at 97 percent, followed by Boston College (94), Rice (93) and Duke (92).

In all sports, Notre Dame had the highest percentage of programs with a perfect 100 GSR rating, including both men's and women's basketball, hockey, baseball, both men's and women's cross country/track, men's and women's fencing, men's and women's golf, women's lacrosse, women's rowing, men's and women's soccer, women's softball, men's and women's swimming, women's tennis and women's volleyball.

The reach of the program has been felt well beyond Notre Dame.

DeCicco's pioneering advisory program became the model for countless other colleges and universities as well as positioning Notre Dame as the leader in showing how athletics and academics could be mutually supportive and beneficial. The pinnacle of that success came in 1988 when Notre Dame became the nation's first football national champion ever to boast a 100-percent graduation rate.

The majority of National Collegiate Athletic Association

schools now have some sort of academic advising program in place. The NCAA itself has also adopted new standards designed to combat exploitation and help scholarship athletes get the education they have been promised.

In 2003, the NCAA created the Academic Progress Rate, which holds Division I institutions accountable for the academic progress of their student-athletes through a team-based metric. Every Division I sports team calculates its APR each academic year based on the eligibility, graduation and retention of each scholarship student-athlete. Teams scoring below certain thresholds can face consequences, such as practice restrictions and restrictions on postseason competition.

In 2012, the NCAA Executive Committee approved $4.8 million in funding for three years for a pilot program that will help Division I schools identified as "limited-resource" institutions develop systems to increase their student-athletes' academic performance. The funding is in addition to $4 million allocated to the Division I Supplemental Support Fund, which was established in 2007, and has allowed many schools to add academic advisors and counselors, provide laptops to student-athletes to use while they travel to games, and upgrade study hall areas, computer labs and other academic study space.

Many outside Notre Dame circles still do not know that it was DeCicco who started this academic movement. In fact, some of his achievements in the field have only recently come to light.

In 2002, DeCicco was inducted into the National Italian

American Sports Hall of Fame, and in 2009 he was the recipient of the Moose Krause Distinguished Service Award. The Moose Krause award, named for the late Notre Dame Athletic Director, is the highest honor given by the Monogram Club. It is awarded to a club member, in part, for their dedication to the spirit and ideals of Notre Dame, which DeCicco had in abundance.

"He always had a big heart," his daughter Linda DeCicco said earlier this year. "It's true. Just ask his cardiologist."

DeCicco's health had been in decline, and a few months later that big heart took its final beats. Mike DeCicco passed away at 4:30 p.m. on Friday, March 29, 2013, from congestive heart failure at Holy Cross Village at Notre Dame. He was 85 years old.

Friends, family and hundreds of student-athletes past and present came to the Notre Dame campus the morning of April 3, 2013, for DeCicco's Funeral Mass at the Basilica of the Sacred Heart. When the mourners emerged from the service—led by his beloved Polly and the DeCicco family—more than 50 fencers were waiting with their weapons held in salute, forming a canopy for their former coach.

At the reception that followed, 26 people spoke and the tributes lasted 90 minutes. Words like "pillar" and "icon" were used with frequency. They were words DeCicco would never use to describe himself.

DeCicco was laid to rest at Cedar Grove Cemetery, but

the true monument to his life will forever rest in the generations of student-athletes that received a true education and earned a degree from the University of Notre Dame.

ACKNOWLEDGEMENTS

WRITING THIS BOOK would have been impossible without considerable assistance from the DeCicco family. I am deeply indebted to Mike DeCicco for the time he spent with me in the final months of a remarkable life. I am equally indebted to his beloved Polly, and children Linda, Michele, Nick, Della, and Michael, who shared personal stories and provided access to numerous articles and personal photos as well as a wealth of detailed information from Linda's genealogical research.

Special gratitude is owed to the Rev. Theodore M. Hesburgh, C.S.C., for his words, wisdom and blessing, and to the memory of the late Rev. Ned Joyce, whose character and leadership played an essential role in the telling of this story.

I am grateful to the leadership team and donors of the 1966 Notre Dame National Championship Football Team Charitable Fund, whose fundraising efforts made this project possible, particularly Dan Harshman '68, who was always there to reach out to various sources throughout the Notre Dame community and showed, on more than one occasion, that he could have a promising second career conducting interviews himself; and Ron Jeziorski '67, who not only aided in that capacity but whose enthusiasm and original idea of honoring Mike DeCicco's legacy served as the guiding light for this project. Thanks is also owed to the other members of the book committee: Brian Boulac '63, Frank Criniti '69, Jack Donahue '67, Jerry Kelly '67, Professor Bill Leahy '56, John Lium '67, and Mike Sullivan '79.

Special appreciation for their generous contributions goes to Harry Alexander; Robert Belden; Larry Conjar; William Daddio; Louis Fournier; Bill Giles; Dave Haley; Terry Hanratty; Kevin Hardy; Mike Heaton; Michael Holtzapfel; John Horney; Robert Jockish; Jim Kelly; Rudy Konieczny; Bob Kuechenberg; Peter Lamantia; Jim Lynch; Joe Marsico; David Martin; Joel Maturi; Mike McCoy; Mike McGill; Jack Meyer; Leonard Moretti, Jr.; Joseph O'Neill; Coley O'Brien; Alan Page; Ara Parseghian; John Pergine; Steve Quinn; Thomas Quinn; John Raniere, Jr.; Kevin Rassas; Tom Rhoades; Angelo Schiralli; Jack Sullivan; Dick Swatland; and Timothy Sweeney. Appreciation also goes to John and Wendy Bognar and Don and Susie Laurie for their support.

I would like to thank Notre Dame's entire fencing community, especially Mike Sullivan, Jeff Pero and Molly Sullivan Sliney, as well as Walter Langford's son, Jim Langford at Corby Publishing, for the opportunity to tell this tale.

Important contributions were also made by Lou Holtz; Gerry Faust; Roger Valdiserri; Sharon Leahy Sullivan; Jim Gunshinan; Luis O. Krug; Heather McGurdy; Pierre du Vair; and Tim Glass.

I benefited from the published work of journalists Kerry Temple; Liz Michalski; Kerry Drohan; Dan McGrath; Herman Weiskopf; Eddie White; Herb Gould; Michael Haggerty; and Brian Burnsed.

I am forever grateful to my wife, Karyn Lewis Bonfiglio, for providing love, encouragement, and for unofficially editing this book with skill and care; and our son, William, for reminding me of the importance of stepping away to go play outside. I am eternally indebted to my father, the late James D. Bonfiglio, for always encouraging me to follow my own path and introducing me to Notre Dame athletics, and to my mother, Peggy Bonfiglio, for reading countless bedtime stories and sharing her love for the written word.

For providing friendship and sage counsel, I must thank James Pickering; the late Dave Rumbach; and John Sparks.

For inspiration in all its forms, I am thankful for the words of Nick Hornby; F. Scott Fitzgerald; Jon Krakauer; Hunter S. Thompson; Charles Bukowski; and Declan MacManus; and for the lessons learned at my own beloved alma mater, Eastern Kentucky University.

APPENDIX

> The idea for this book started as a conversation between Ron Jeziorski and John Lium who were looking for a way to honor the legacy of Coach Mike DeCicco. The first thought was to solicit letters from some of the student-athletes who Coach DeCicco had helped over the years. Although the project evolved from there, many of those letters became the basis for the stories told in this book. The following is a sampling of some of the letters.

A Man for All Seasons.

That's exactly what Mike DeCicco was. Everyone that came into contact with Mike knew how important he was to the entire Notre Dame Athletic program. He handled all of the sports while still coaching the Notre Dame fencing team to 5 national championships and continued teaching in the Engineering College.

When I first came to Notre Dame in 1964, I was introduced to Mike and the academic program he headed at the University. He originally started for the football team and the need for his work became very apparent. It expanded into all of the varsity sports because of the continued requirement to make progress toward a degree and obviously eligibility for participation. Even though the screening process for enrollment is a rigorous one, some students may be weak in one or two subjects and need guidance and tutorial help. This is where Mike's

program excelled. His input on the athletes he guided
are well documented with letters from his former students
acknowledging the benefits they had received from Mike's
attention to their academic needs.

Mike had the support of all of the coaches. They
had great respect for his guidance of their athletic
students. Personally I had a very strong and close relationship with Mike. If a coach doesn't cooperate with the
academic advisor and respond to the counselors he or she
can possibly lose a top athlete.

There is no question in my mind that our football
program would not have been as successful without Mike
DeCicco's academic input. There are countless examples of
a player being weak in 1 or 2 subjects that additional
help from a tutor made the difference in his entire
college life and future. He was a father figure to the
players—helping them make the academic adjustments necessary. These are so important particularly to incoming
freshmen and following them through to graduation. It is
so obvious when the players return to campus for reunions
the respect they show to Mike. They never fail to stop by
and express their admiration for his guidance. Yes, Mike
was a man for all seasons. You can ask any of his former
student athletes.

Ara Parseghian

December 15, 2005

Coach Michael DeCicco
125 Joyce Center
Notre Dame, Indiana 46556-5678

Dear Coach:

When I returned to campus last year after an absence
of many years, I was surprised and very pleased to find
my photograph displayed in the Joyce Center. But the
pleasure of that discovery paled in comparison to the joy
of unexpectedly seeing you and Polly in the fencing room
and the delight of spending time with both of you. I've
thought often about those events of last year and it's
hard for me to express adequately in words how much it
means to me that both you and Notre Dame have remembered
me after the passage of so many years.

I will never be able to repay you, the fencing team
and Notre Dame for all that I was so blessed to receive
during my time at Notre Dame. As you know, I have sup-
ported the fencing team for many years through contributions to the Fencing Endowment Fund and its predecessor
fund. I have realized as a result of my recent visit to
Notre Dame and the time I spent with you and Polly while
I was there, however, that I want to do more. Consequently, I have decided to endow a permanent fencing scholarship through a contribution of $100,000 to Notre Dame over
the course of the next several years. I understand that
it will be only the second endowed athletic scholarship
at Notre Dame and I am pleased that it will benefit future
Notre Dame fencers.

During my years at Notre Dame, you encouraged and
inspired me to excel in both athletics and academics.
I remember well that during the fencing team's visit to
Chicago for a meet during my senior year, you arranged
for the team bus driver to drive me, on the team bus,
to an interview with a federal judge. Your thoughtful
gesture reduced the anxiety of that important step in
the competitive process of applying for a substantial law

school scholarship which I ultimately received. Your support of my efforts to succeed both on and off the fencing strip helped me build the foundation for a future that ultimately enabled and inspired me to endow the fencing scholarship.

I am writing to let you know how much you and Notre Dame continue to mean to me and of my efforts, through my support of the fencing program, to return some of the blessings you have conferred upon so many fencers who have been privileged to call you "Coach."

Warmest regards,
Jeff Pero

Sometime in 1963 as I recall, our brilliant football coaching staff decided that a tutoring program would be helpful to the athletes because of the time demands of football and frequent travel. Mike DeCicco, at that time an accounting professor, as I remember it, was selected to run the tutoring program. All football players were invited to participate either as a pupil for free or an instructor with pay of $4.75 an hour (could have been lower). Since my strengths ran more to the mental side of the game, I volunteered to be an instructor. I received a call shortly thereafter from a Sophomore who was willing to try the new medicine. He came to my room one evening and we proceeded to learn. The subject was statistics and the first problem the student had was a severe dislike of the subject. We proceeded to learn that it could be valuable in later life, had practical applications, and might even help in successful play selection.

Once the student gained an interest in statistics, he was showing me how great it was now that he had seen the light. I wish a could say that I saw a brilliant playing career ahead for this gentleman, but I did not. I only saw him as a future "A" student. Because of his quick grasp of the subject matter, he never returned as a pupil. As for his playing career, I had failed to understand how this newfound knowledge of statistics would rocket this pupil into the best football player of the 1964 season, Heisman Trophy winner, John Huarte.

Thanks to Coach DeCicco for his organizational skills, his dedication to the welfare of student athletes, and his foresightedness in making this program a success. The University could not have picked a better man for the job!!

> Thanks, Coach,
> Joe Monahan '64 – football

A NOTRE DAME MAN

The first time I competed for ND and gave up a touch.... I heard that coming from the end of the strip. Pretty good advice for athletics, pretty good advice for life.

As a freshman, I remember going over and just sitting in his office and listening to all the different conversations. Coach D, always colorful, and never boring, was a pretty scary character for my first couple of seasons at ND. He was always the example of the right thing to do, as that was his mantra in everything he talked about.

Junior year, as a captain, I got summoned more times than I care to count and I did as much talking (explaining) as listening. As I got older he demanded more in terms of leadership and responsibility, and I found that he listened more.

Senior year, I was so very proud to be part of our first NCAA Championship. It is one of the highlights of my fencing career, ranking right up there with my Olympic Team membership and individual national and international medals.

I firmly believe that none of those accomplishments would have occurred without Coach.

Of course, he is TOTALLY responsible for the direction my life has gone. He got me accepted into ND (not that I would have gone anywhere else). I met my wife, Marie, at ND. We are blessed with 4 children (2 of them are ND grads and our youngest will start in August).

Needless to say, I am just one of many that Coach DeCicco has had a positive influence on, both at ND and beyond.

                    THANKS, COACH!
                    Tim Glass '77 - fencing

I have to say my memories of fencing and my time with Coach DeCicco are among the best...if not THE best...memories of Notre Dame. He not only taught me everything I learned about fencing but imbued a sense of honor and hard work and integrity that, hopefully, has not faded. I remember his admonition that it was not about winning but about "how" we won and how we treated our opponents and how we represented ND that would really make our mark, long after Win-Loss records faded.

Since graduation, I went on to medical school and became an ER physician. After 9-11, I entered the US Navy and was assigned as a battalion surgeon for a Marine Infantry unit. I had two deployments overseas, the last to Afghanistan where I took care of many injured Marines and local villagers. I am back home now...with my wife and 6 children...but the memories of Notre Dame and Coach have never left me of course ...and never will.

Thank you, Coach!
Roy Seitz '74 – fencing

A NOTRE DAME MAN

August 20, 2012

When I arrived on campus as a freshman, Coach immediately made me feel at home. Being a New Yorker, I learned I could poke some fun at his Jersey heritage. I grew up amongst Italian families from our neighborhood and parish. I told him Filipinos and Italians are a lot alike: big voices, big appetites, big faith, big family, and big heart. My maiden name, Garcia, ends in a vowel, so he said I was "Good." Coach raised the fencers as a family. I loved "family dinner" at Bruno's. I always felt safe, loved, and respected by the coaches and my teammates. For many of us, the fencing team was our niche in the Notre Dame community and an invaluable part of our Notre Dame experience.

At the end of sophomore year, I was elected to be captain of the women's foil team starting the fall of junior year. When the outgoing captains announced the results, I immediately thought there was a mistake. I met with Coach and told him I didn't know why they elected me and that I didn't think I could do it. He told me that was horse you know-what. He also told me that good leaders always have a little bit of doubt, but a wealth of faith. He told me I'm a rich young woman and others are hoping for me to draw on that faith to lead them. He believed in and respected me even when I was not confident with myself. I served as captain my junior and senior year and we brought home the NCAA title during the latter in 1994. He always inspired me to work hard; the effort alone always made him proud.

My junior and senior year he helped me work towards my other dream of being a physician. He wrote an amazing number of letters of recommendation. He called alumni to mentor me and he encouraged me every day to strive for my dream. When I received my acceptance into graduate school for public health and then medical school, I knew I could not have done it without him. He was Professor DeCicco as much as he was Coach DeCicco; he was Superman!

When we returned to campus after winning the NCAA title my senior year, I sobbed realizing that my time with the Notre Dame Fencing Team was approaching an end. Being a part of this amazing team made my Notre Dame experience one to remember for a lifetime. I started dating my husband, Brian, second semester senior year. When I brought him to the fencing gym to meet Coach I had the same excitement and fear as when I introduced Brian to my parents. I highly respected Coach's opinion. He had become such an integral part of my life; he truly was my family.

In 1996, Coach was the US Representative for the Olympic Fencing Team. At the time I had just finished graduate school and was starting medical school at Emory University in Atlanta. I got to see him in action again, but at the Olympics. He took me to the events and, of course, to dinner. It was the most welcomed break from the rigors of medical school. Getting a dose of Notre Dame spirit and love brought much comfort during that challenging time. He told me to study hard and to use my God-given gifts to the fullest. He told me he had no doubts that I would finish my studies because I was meant to help others. After conversations with him I always knew things were going to be alright.

Every fall we return to Notre Dame for a football game. We do our usual pilgrimage to the fencing gym to visit "The Don." Per his advice, we make the Grotto our first and last destination with a visit to the fencing gym (and oh, yeah, a football game, too) thrown in between. It's truly a homecoming when we are able to see him those weekends.

I could go on and on. The experience of writing this letter is bittersweet. I love Coach DeCicco. Simply put , he's the best.

Dinamarie ("Didi") Garcia-Banigan, MD, MPH
Notre Dame '94 – fencing

As a member of the fencing team my interaction with Coach Mike DeCicco was a major part of my Notre Dame experience. However one brief but formative interaction stands out in my mind. I was an Arts and Letters pre-professional student aiming for a career in medicine. I was on track with adequate grades to be admitted to medical school except for one little problem—French. The specific problem was the oral competency exam in a foreign language required to graduate from Notre Dame in the College of Arts and Letters. My written French was fine, but my oral French was abysmal, and I flunked the exam.

I needed help for the makeup exam and I stopped by Coach's office to see if he could help. I was not calm. In probably less than 30 minutes he assured me that he could arrange for whatever tutoring was required to improve my French. His manner was calm and reassuring enough that I was able to eventually pass the exam and finish the semester with a "B." I might have been admitted to medical school anyway but I am not at all certain of it. I will always remember his help at a time when I really needed it. I'd like to think that my work as a physician has done some good but it might never have been possible without Coach DeCicco.

John H. Isaacs, MD FACS '71 - fencing

I had one and exactly one meeting with Mike DeCicco. It wasn't really a meeting "with" Mr. DeCicco. Rather it was what, in retrospect, must have been an incoming freshman hazing, I mean "orientation" session. Over the course of a meeting that was much longer than any student found comfortable (lest we catch his attention in some unsuspecting way), he completely scared the heck out of everyone in the room. No question about it—we were to get our academic work done. And if we didn't, he would know about it; he would find us; and we would pay a significant unknown price. I left convinced I had better do just as he said. I never again met "with" Mr. DeCicco.

Stephen G. Welch '79 - track

A NOTRE DAME MAN

I'll never forget the day I met Coach DeCicco.
It was in the fall of my Freshman year (1977). I had
recently been "cut" from the Marching Band—which is
another story in and of itself. Nevertheless, I was
walking back to Zahm Hall with Sal Mouio, a fellow "Zah-
mie" who was in most of my freshman Engineering classes.
On our way back to the dorm, Sal asked if I would mind
stopping at the Main Building with him so that he could
pick something up from Coach DeCicco's office (which,
at the time, was on the third floor, right around the
corner from Fr. Hesburgh's office). When we stopped in,
Sal introduced me to Coach as "Jimmy Sullivan, from New
Hampshire." When Coach heard that, he asked if my father
had attended Notre Dame. When I said, "Yes," he started
telling me about my dad. For example, he knew that my
father had been a boxer. (He actually won the Super
Featherweight title in the 1947 Bengal Bouts.) How weird
was that? As it turns out, Coach DeCicco and my father
were classmates at ND. At that moment, he treated me as
though we were related. He told me that I should join
the Freshman Fencing team. I really had no idea what
fencing was but Coach's aura made it seem like it must
be the most wonderful sport in the world. So, I signed
up. Little did I know, that was the start of the single
most defining factor in my Notre Dame career.

I started out struggling in Engineering and, unlike
Sal, who ultimately switched majors and became a very
successful finance guy in New York City, I was determined
to survive as an engineer. Coach DeCicco's mentoring,
both in the gym and from his office, made all the difference in the world. When I was on the verge of academic
peril, he made sure that I succeeded. As an example,
I was never a stellar calculus student. In fact, that
was my single worst subject at ND. During my freshman year, I had a professor from Eastern Europe whom
I could barely understand. Of course, since calculus
is difficult to understand anyway, it didn't make for
such a good combination. So, I pretty much bombed both
semesters—barely passing, by the skin of my teeth. When
I arrived for Calc Ill, at the beginning of sophomore
year, I found myself in a class led by another "foreign"
professor (who actually got his foot stuck in the trash

can in the classroom on that first day of class). I knew
I was doomed. As soon as class was dismissed, I marched
myself right over to Coach's office. When I explained my
predicament, he said not to worry, picked up the phone
and dialed the Chairman of the Math Department. The
next thing I knew, I had been transferred to the Chairman's Calc III section. I never excelled at Calculus
but I managed to improve my grade to a "B-" for both
Calc III and IV. Coach never "spoon-fed" anybody but he
helped everyone get the tools they needed to be able to
succeed on their own. He was the same way in the fencing gym.

Back in my day, fencing was a different animal at
Notre Dame. We didn't have any Olympic fencers on the
team. Sure we had "stars" —like Mike Sullivan, who had
fencing careers where you could count the number of
bouts that they actually lost (in four years) on a single
hand. In the late 1970's, fencing wasn't a big high school
sport in the United States. There were, however, a few
areas in the US where kids did have the opportunity to
fence in high school but that was pretty much confined
to Boston, New York, Chicago and California. So, there
were always a number of us who started fencing in college. (Could you even imagine that today? It seems as
though kids have to choose which sport they want to play
when they are in grade school and concentrate on that
sport and that sport alone—if they want to even hope to
have an opportunity to compete at the collegiate level.)
Even though we were newcomers to the sport, none of
the "stars" ever treated us like we were anything other
than critical members of the team. That attribute came
directly from Coach. In his eyes, we were more than a
team—we were a family. We all played our part. Like a
play, some teammates had the leading roles, some had
supporting roles and a whole bunch more were in the
ensemble. Yet, we all worked in harmony as a cohesive
unit to achieve extraordinary results. In fact, as I
reminisce, my "role" was really a glorified pin cushion.
After a while, I realized that I had developed a "pretty
good hand," which meant I began reacting pretty instinc-
tively to moves made against me. (That's just a nice way
of saying that I was a sucker.) What that translated

into was that I made a pretty realistic practice dummy.
Our more accomplished fencers could "drill" with me
and I would react appropriately to their faints—giving
them the opportunity to hone their moves to perfection.
I never became a star on the team but I like to think
that I still played an important part in our success.
During my sophomore year, I started practicing regularly
with a foilist named Andy Bonk, who hailed from Park
Ridge, Illinois. Every Monday – Friday, Andy and I would
meet at the fencing gym at 3:00—an hour before practice
officially started. We ran through drills over and over
until 4:00, when we would merge into the team practice
that continued until around 6:00, giving us barely
enough time to clean up and run across campus to the
dining hall for dinner. (In those days, only the football and basketball teams had the luxury of "training
tables" for dinner. While our team finished 2nd at the
NCAA Championship that year, Andy did win the NCAA foil
championship. It was such an honor to have been able to
help out—even if it was merely by having a permanent
bruise on my chest that school year. So, I made my mark,
albeit in the background—just as my image appears in a
photograph of Andy that hangs in the fencing display in
the JACC. Standing in the background, behind the face of
Andy, is a much younger (and much thinner) "me," pres-
sure-testing the tip of one of Andy's weapons . (Dean
Merten, our armorer, taught me how to heat-treat the
springs that are in the tips of foils and epees to make
sure they were "legal" but only barely so. That way,
Andy never had to worry that his weapon wouldn't regis-
ter a legitimate touch.)

The discipline that was required to succeed as
a student athlete has served me well in life. Having
demanding commitments taught me valuable time management skills. Practicing for three hours a day forced me
to spend the time I had between classes in the library,
completing homework assignments or studying for exams. I
would also have to plan my days ahead of time, assemble
everything I needed and put my nose to the grindstone.
That's pretty much what I've been doing for the past 30
years of my professional career.

Jim Sullivan '81 – fencing

My path to ND fencing was atypical—I learned to fence in the PE program my freshman year. After winning the NVA tournament, I met Coach DeCicco and learned about ND's "novice" tradition. I found a fencing club near my home that summer and prepared to try to make the team my sophomore year. The season began with a picnic at Coach's home. I was astonished to see this legendary man open his home to us; this was my first view into ND fencing and I was so excited. He and his wife Polly could not have been nicer. I quickly learned that this would not be my "sport," my "activity" or even my "team." This was a family.

Despite the fact that I was not an extraordinary fencer (my career record was only 16-3), Coach always made me feel like I was truly part of the team, and that my growth and success were as important to him as to the myriad All-Americans on squad. He always took time to instruct not just about fencing but about how to treat others and how to make our way through life. I was even fortunate enough my senior year to receive a sabre lesson from him—a memory I'll cherish forever.

The most important thing I learned from Coach (other than some colorful phrases about the various uses for a rusty sabre) was to treat all people with kindness regardless of their state or status. As a novice on the team I expected to be relegated to second-tier status. Instead, I always felt included as part of the team and learned a great deal that I keep with me as I go through life.

        Jim Kowalski '89 - fencing

A NOTRE DAME MAN

Coach DeCicco literally changed the course of my life. I'm not sure what course I was on—drifting down the stream I guess—when a decision Coach made led me to ND. If I remember correctly, the 1988 Junior World Fencing Championships had been scheduled for Beirut and then were moved to Sydney for security reasons, but Sydney pulled out the year before they were to be held and Coach DeCicco, in typical style, stepped forward and offered to hold them in South Bend at the University of Notre Dame. I was lucky enough to make the Australian team for that event and was thus in the US in the early months of 1988. One thing led to another and suddenly, with Coach's intervention, I was meeting with the ND admissions office and studying for the SATs. An unexpected turn of events for an Aussie girl from the Gold Coast who wasn't sure where life was heading! Jump forward to August 1988 and I arrived at ND by bus to start freshman year on a fencing scholarship, the beginning of an amazing four years in my life. In that four years I studied hard, I worked hard, I trained hard, I competed hard and I grew beyond belief.

After a freshman year working part-time in a typical freshman job (cashiering evenings at South Dining Hall), Coach bailed me out again, giving me a part-time job in the Office of Academic Advising which he had founded and run for many years. The hours spent in that office during the following three years helped earn me spending money and provided me with lots of unexpected but invaluable mentoring from the team there and gave me some amazing insights into helping students find balance, in this case between being elite athletes and achieving academically.

Neither Coach nor I could have predicted then that my part-time student role in the Office would prepare me well for my early career in academic administration back in Australia, where I applied much that I had seen and heard in the Office to my role as academic adviser in the School of Humanities & Social Sciences at Bond University, a role which launched my career in international education. I haven't looked back and I haven't forgotten the fundamentals I learned in that office.

I recently returned to ND for my 20-year reunion, looking forward to catching up with my Lewis Hall dorm-mates only to realize that most of the students who were really significant in my Notre Dame life were my fencing teammates. When I ran into some of them at reunion it felt like coming home. I didn't expect it but I should have known that the group I shared five afternoons a week, most weekends and countless road trips with were my real Notre Dame family...with the indomitable Coach as the head of family.

When I think about Coach a regular series of im-ages and sounds goes through my head: The love of his life, Polly; Coach saying "Jesus, Joseph & Mary"; Coach threatening to tear some young punk a new one with a rusty sabre; Joe Montana (roommate to Coach's son as an undergrad and lifelong friend to Coach); Coach's love of family; Coach's love of Notre Dame; and Coach's love of us—in many ways a strange and international band of mis-fits drawn together through a love for our sport. I also think of food. The fencing team was highly envied for the meals we had on the road and closer to home—Bruno's in South Bend, Ed Debevicks and deep dish pizza in Chicago, amazing Amish food. The football team's weekly surf and turf meals weren't a patch on the wonderful meals shared by the ND Fencing Team.

Coach is synonymous with Notre Dame for me. If it weren't for him I never would have been at ND and I most certainly wouldn't have achieved everything I did in my four years there. There wasn't a fencer who didn't love him and, although we weren't the only ones to benefit from Coach's long career at ND, we certainly got the best of him and are all the richer for it. I love you Coach!

Heidi Piper '92 - fencing

A NOTRE DAME MAN

My story about Mike DeCicco is not heroic but his influence had far reaching impact on me and many fellow athletes back in the 1972-1976 timeframe. I was a Baseball recruit and four year-varsity player, who came to Notre Dame without scholarship and in a Mechanical Engineering curriculum. Scared to death, I looked for any resource to help me get off to a good start, arrange compatible schedules, and assure I managed my way through all the core requirements and electives during my four years at ND. Coach DeCicco was always there to help regardless of the sport or your standing in or out of the starting lineup. I also think he had a soft spot in his heart for Engineers and Architects, as he hailed from the School of Architecture. Senior year, my schedule allowed for one technical elective and I managed my way into Coach DeCicco's Heating, Ventilation, and Air Conditioning (HVAC) course intended for the less technical Architecture candidates. I was ever grateful for that grade of "A" which helped me on my way to a 3.0 GPA and an on-time graduation in May, 1976. Certainly not the top of the class, but a proud moment for me nonetheless.

I am now a 36-year veteran of E.I. DuPont de Nemours & Company. Ten moves later, I have worked my way through assignments in Operations, Engineering, Human Resources, Labor Relations, R&D, Marketing, Sales, and finally Business Management. I look back to my Notre Dame years with fond memories and a debt of gratitude to people like Mike DeCicco, Emil Hofman, Jake Kline, Tom Kelly, Rev. Robert Griffin, and Rev. Ted Hesburgh who taught us about time management, adaptability, discipline, hard work, dedication, ethics, and a special kindness to help others grow and succeed in life.

Dave Lazzeri '76 - baseball
MBA '84 U of Detroit

Mike had a profound impact on my academic career without ever having spoken with him. As a freshman I went to his office during the third week of school to ask him if I could drop a class. I was finding that schoolwork was occupying way too much time and was interfering with my football pursuits. As I took a seat in the waiting room I looked to my left and noticed that Mike's office door was ajar enough that I could clearly hear voices and witness a life-changing event.

Mike had crossed swords mounted on the wall behind his desk, I assumed as a symbol of his affection for fencing. Within two minutes of my entering the waiting room, Mike jumped up from his desk, grabbed one of the swords off the wall and pointed it at the throat of my nameless teammate and yelled, "If you cut one more class, I'll take care of you with this rusty saber!" At that time I realized that academics at Notre Dame were a priority. That was the only motivation I needed. I quickly exited the Administration Building and went directly to the library without Mike knowing I had been there.

Ken MacAfee '78 — football

My biggest remembrance of the academic services was this.

First, we were informed that the academics were going to be taken seriously. Do it or go home. After that, we still were in contact with the offices and the staff people like "Bert" Goodson, who stayed up on our progress. It was the relationships that always made the difference.

Second, "Coach" Bill Leahy gave me some great advice, and that was to begin my major early, when I was a freshman. This early start allowed me more flexibility in taking classes that matched my needs and wants later in my junior and senior years.

Dave Casper '74 football

Coach DeCicco was a significant help to me throughout my four years at Notre Dame and someone that I greatly respect. I can recall meeting with him on several occasions to review my academic progress. He inspired me to become more serious about my education and to put forth a greater effort in the classroom. I was fortunate enough to go on to earn an MBA from Northwestern University. As a result, many career opportunities became open to me and I owe him a tremendous debt of gratitude. He has had a major impact on my life and countless other ND athletes. On a broader front, Coach DeCicco was instrumental in laying the foundation for the positive student-athlete image Notre Dame enjoys to this day.

Kevin Rassas '68 - football

Although I did not utilize the tutoring sessions, I served as a calculus tutor during the 1990-1991 school year. During that time, I worked with several football and tennis athletes.

One thing that stands out to me—a high school teacher of 18 years—as I reflect back on that time period is how important it was for that program to exist. First, the time commitment for a Division I athlete under any circumstances would be overwhelming. The expectation for excellence on the field at the University of Notre Dame has always been second to none. For a young man who is transitioning to the college academic expectations, that must have been even more overwhelming. How many Division I football teams are part of a university that expects each student—YES EACH STUDENT—to take two semesters of calculus regardless of major? Coach D's program provided that safety net that did not just aid in calculus instruction, but helped model quality study habits that would not have necessarily been instilled at the high school level.

Another factor that stands out to me is related to the two semesters of calculus requirement. Two athletes came to mind when I was writing the previous paragraph—Chris Zorich and Aaron Taylor. These two young men came from urban environments and, although they were bright enough guys and had outstanding work ethics, they were enrolled in classes with people who had significantly stronger math backgrounds. What I loved about Coach D's program was that athletes like this were paired up with people who could help build the athletes' confidence and competence in calculus through modeling the various types of problems. I can't imagine how difficult it would be for young men like that prior to the program. Many would have resorted to cheating. One of my fondest memories of being a "budding teacher" as a tutor in the program was the day I saw Aaron Taylor walking back to his dorm after his calculus final and receiving a GIANT hug for the help I had provided throughout the semester. As a student-athlete myself, I gained confidence in my love of teaching. For Aaron, calculus might have been just one battle in the war to achieve a degree from the

University of Notre Dame, but it was a major stepping stone in his building of academic confidence. Coach D's program provided the transition to academic life that was desperately needed for these young men and women who had never experienced the intensity of Division I academic and athletic demands—particularly in their freshman years.

Heather "Casey" McCurdy '93 - softball

A NOTRE DAME MAN

I still vividly remember making a recruiting trip to Notre Dame in the winter of 1980. My friends back at home were giving me a hard time about going to cold Indiana when I had the opportunity to play baseball for a school down in the south. I remember "if you want to play in cold weather, stay closer to home," which was 50 miles outside of Boston. I listened but still made the trip because "it was Notre Dame." It was not known for baseball but I was still intrigued.

I was treated with the utmost respect during my recruiting trip. I saw the campus even though it was slightly snow covered. I got to spend quality time with baseball coach Larry Gallo (with whom I still remain in contact) and the team. I got to meet Digger and the basketball team—I realize today that was a move to expose me to more diversity on campus and make me feel more comfortable. Also, like many recruits, I was able to attend a hall dance and see the social side of college living.

But here I am 32 years later, and the number one thing that still stands out for me on that recruiting trip was the time spent with Coach Mike DeCicco and his staff learning about the student-athlete academic advisory program and how assistance was available, if needed. The University of Notre Dame spent more time with me on that trip discussing academics as opposed to athletics—a distinction that really stood out for me at that time comparing it to other universities. Because of that, I felt like I "just fit" at Notre Dame and decided to attend. And the fact that my father was a subway alum did not hurt either.

So whether he knows it or not, Coach DeCicco was a great influence on me in making one of life's toughest decisions when you are 17 years old. And for that, I say thank you.

Having been a part of the Monogram Club for several years, I had the opportunity to see The Monogram Club honor Coach DeCicco...an honor to this day that is the most deserved.

Sincerely,
Bob (Buster) Lopes '85 - baseball

Up until I was 18 years old I knew Mike DeCicco as Uncle Mike, Polly DeCicco as Aunt Polly, and the DeCicco children (Michele, Linda, Nick, Della, and Mike junior) as my Midwestern cousins who would show up for family reunions in Maryland, where I grew up, and impress all us easterners with how nice they were—my first experience of Indiana nice. But Uncle Mike was the loudest of a set of pretty loud uncles and said things that made us blush a little bit, but laugh hard. I've since found out that the Indiana nice I experienced is deep down and genuine.

Polly and her brothers and sisters grew up with my Mom and her brothers and sister above a country store in a small town in West Virginia, but I'll leave that story to others.

When I sat down with the DeCiccos during freshman orientation week, Mike asked me what kind of extracurricular activities interested me. I said I was thinking about crew. Uncle Mike said, "What about fencing?" I knew he was a coach of a strange sport that I knew nothing about, but I had no idea I could actually participate in it. For the next four years I would call him Coach. If I had any thought of special treatment, those thoughts would have been banished within a few months. I spent a year going to the gym four nights a week learning the basics on the Novice Team. I joined the varsity team sophomore year and provided a target all year for the more experienced fencers. Junior year I got better than most of Notre Dame's lesser opponents and earned my Monogram. Senior year I was a starter on the Epee squad.

I learned from Coach to set goals. I set realistic goals each year and I met them. I learned to work hard and to combine that work ethic with a positive sense of my potential. Coach told me that he really liked the fencers who "talk a good game," even if they weren't the most naturally gifted. "If they say they'll do it, there is a good chance they will do it." I learned that a good coach knows each team member as an individual, with individual needs and ways of being motivated. I think he figured out the best way to motivate me was to ignore me most of the time (unless I was with the DeCiccos at a family celebration, when he became my uncle again and bragged about me being a fencer). He knew that I was the kind of guy who wanted to please his teachers and coaches, and that I would provide most of my own motivation. When he did speak well of me as a fencer (he said once that I had a "stellar career"), I would fly high for days.

I've had some time to get to know him better as an uncle and as a man after I graduated, came back to Notre Dame for grad school, and for eight years while I was working in South Bend. I lived with Polly and Mike for two weeks once when I was going through a personal crisis. They let me be when I needed solitude but then we talked a lot about life in the evening while eating non-fat yogurt ice cream.

I know Coach poured his heart and soul into his coaching and academic advising, and that his family sometimes felt neglected because of it. I know his life would have been different if he had stayed in Newark, New Jersey, where he grew up—most of his friends there, he told me once, were either dead or in jail—or if he had chosen a more lucrative career in private industry. He wanted to be a part of the life of Notre Dame. I think he was realistic. He knew the place wasn't perfect. But he believed in Father Hesburgh and Father Joyce, and the vision they had for Notre Dame as a whole, and for the athletic programs. My Aunt Polly also told him early on that she wanted to stay in South Bend. She thought it would be a good place to raise their family. And it was.

Jim Gunshinan '81 - fencing

I attended Notre Dame from 1975 to 1979 and had the privilege to know Coach DeCicco under a variety of circumstances. In my freshman year, I was an athletic manager and, as such, was assigned to assist at the practices of the various sports. During a football practice at Cartier Field, I had been instructed that a certain area near the field was a restricted area and no one was allowed to enter. While completing my duties, I was directed by the Head Manager to contact a man in the restricted area and ask him to leave. I approached the man and politely asked him to move to another location. He just as politely told me that he had no intention of moving. I returned to the Head Manager and explained the situation. I was once again told to ask the man to move, but it was déjà vu. After a third attempt also failed, the Head Manager personally contacted the man, who then agreed to move elsewhere. Upon my asking who the man was, the Head Manager replied, "Coach Mike DeCicco." When I suggested that this Coach DeCicco was a bit arrogant in thinking the rules did not apply to him, the Head Manager said, "Oh no. He just doesn't want the football team to think they can order everyone around." Thus began my relationship with Coach DeCicco, a man who would have a positive influence on me even after I graduated.

During my sophomore year, I joined Coach DeCicco's Novice Fencing Program. Under the tutelage of a current varsity fencer, I learned to fence. I would later become a 2-year member of the Varsity team. I would sometimes go to Coach DeCicco's office in the Main Administration Building to talk with him about fencing and my plans to graduate and become a high school history teacher. Coach DeCicco was always in the midst of a tempest of activity as he contacted professors, coaches and athletes concerning the athletes' grades prior to preparing to conduct the fencing team practice. Yet he always took time to counsel me, a walk-on, non-scholarship fencer whose highest ranking on the team was second-string.

In my senior year, I got to see how dedicated he was to the success of each and every athlete. I got a message to meet him at his office before practice on a Tuesday afternoon. Not knowing why I was being summoned, I went with trepidation. When I entered his office, he closed the door and said, "I want to talk about your grades. They are slipping and I won't have that." He then went on to explain that I was at Notre Dame for an education, not to just be a fencer. He recounted some of our earlier conversations about how I wanted to be a teacher. He said that every 2 weeks, he would review the athletes' grades and contact professors if necessary. For what seemed like an hour, he advised me about how academics must be my priority and how disappointed he was that I was not achieving at a level he knew I was capable of reaching. Finally, I asked how far my grades had dropped. He replied, "From a 3.5 to a 3.4." I exclaimed, "What would you have done if I had failed?" He had contacted one of my professors, who informed him that I had an exam on Friday. Throughout our conversation, he kept repeating that my grades were dropping, a situation of which I was unaware. He banned me from practice for the next 3 days, even though we had a meet on Saturday and I was on the traveling squad. He said that the professor had agreed to grade my exam immediately and to report my score to Coach DeCicco before fencing practice was scheduled to start. If my exam grade was not acceptable, I would remain on campus over the weekend. I could come to the gym on Friday and learn my fate from the team manager. If the manager was putting together a travel bag for me, then I would go with the team. If the manager was not doing so, I had not done well on the exam and would stay home. Coach DeCicco offered to get a tutor for me or, if necessary, to have someone escort me to the library to ensure that I studied. I told him that neither would be necessary. On Friday morning, I took the exam. In the afternoon I found out I had done well and would be traveling.

I have never forgotten that incident. I could not then, and still cannot now, fathom how much Coach DeCicco must have cared for the athletes if he was willing to go to that extent for me, a guy who had never seen the sport 2 years earlier and who would never become a star athlete for the team. When people complain that college athletes can always loaf in their classes, I tell them I can't speak for every athlete or every school, but I can tell you my story. It is one of the reasons I am so proud to have earned my monogram at Notre Dame.

In one of life's great coincidences, my daughter, who is a junior at Notre Dame, has been working on campus as a tutor for the athletic department. She is carrying on the tradition begun by Coach Mike DeCicco.

Luis O. Krug '79 - fencing

My story is short and sweet but it was a defining moment in my life.

The year is 1978 late in the fall. Coach is looking to establish the starting line-ups before the season starts with the new year.

I had senioritis and was goofing off more than usual.

Coach called a meeting of all the sabre team into his little office off the Fencing Gym...right in the middle of practice. Once we all assembled he turned directly to me and read me the riot act...I was not living up to my potential...I was a disappointment to him...that I had the talent to be a starter but needed to work harder...but worst of all I was letting down all these guys in the room! He then named the starters...not me...you could have heard a pin drop.

We had a great season...I did go to all the meets and did well when called upon.

I replay that moment anytime I get frustrated in life and use it to motivate myself to try harder.

Because I goofed off with my studies too, I did not get into any US Med Schools and had to go to a foreign med school and fight to become a doctor the hard way...but I had Coach DeCicco there in my head anytime I needed the extra motivation.

John P. McGuire MD '79 - fencing

In 1974, I almost dropped out of ND for numerous reasons. The summer of 1974 and the early fall represent one of the most challenging times in my life, yet it also represented one of the greatest growth moments for me.

There are two people who inspired me to stay. The first was Coach Joe Yonto. His talk was exceptional as I reflect back on it. He challenged me.

The other was Coach DeCicco!!! His PUSH, his fire, and yet his smooth style…inspired me to want to stick it out and finish. He always found ways to touch base with me to ensure I never strayed from my focus of finishing up. He is the main reason I completed my degree in Business Administration.

Gene Smith '77 - football

Mike DeCicco was a great coach and mentor for me and I know the advice he gave my classmates and teammates was as instrumental in their success as it was in mine.

My greatest memory of Mike was during my sophomore year at ND when I was taking Professor Walter Langford's Spanish class, a 4-credit course. Professor Langford was a great teacher, but I had always had difficulty learning foreign languages and, despite his efforts, I struggled with the class. In addition to his encouragement, Mike teamed me up with an upperclassman, Chuck (Chico) Reali, whose tutoring and support got me through the class. That was over 45 years ago and I remember it as though it was yesterday. I still dream about those Spanish tests!

Mike DeCicco is one of the reasons why Notre Dame is different than other universities. Mike's objective was not to get you through the course so you could play sports, but rather to succeed as a Notre Dame student. As much as I took pride in my accomplishments as a Notre Dame athlete, I take even more pride in my accomplishment as a Notre Dame graduate. In no short measure, Mike DeCicco helped me to accomplish that dream.

Rudy Konieczny '68 - football

Coach Michael DeCicco has the rare quality to inspire people to achieve beyond their expectations. In spite of Coach's extensive responsibilities at the University of Notre Dame, he found time to welcome many people to participate with his beloved Fencing Program. The Saint Mary's College at Notre Dame Women's Varsity fencers were always appreciative and grateful for Coach's addition in regard to their training, competing and celebrating with the Notre Dame Fencing teams during the 1970s and 1980s. Polly DeCicco attended St. Mary's, and I thank her as well for the priceless opportunities.

During the fall of 1978, I was a first-year Fine Art Major at SMC. The Captain of SMC Women's Fencing Team, Sharon Moore, recruited me to join the ND/SMC Fencing Apprentice Program led by Pat Gerard, ND '78. From Pius X High School in Lincoln, Nebraska, I had 11 Varsity letters in Volleyball, Basketball and Track, achieving the honor of Outstanding Female Athlete my senior year. My schedule at SMC allowed for athletic pursuits, and Sharon's timing was perfect as I had been undecided whether to continue as a student athlete in college. Coach DeCicco generously allowed the SMC Fencers to train at the ACC Notre Dame Fencing gym alongside the ND Women Fencers. At that time women competed only in Foil, so combining our groups for training was a win/win in preparation for competition.

On New Year's Eve 1978 in Dallas, Texas, at the Reunion Hotel, Notre Dame fans gathered the evening before the Cotton Bowl. Walking among the camaraderie of so many ND fans with Judy and Tom Kitchin, my aunt and uncle, my cousins and brother , Mark Kitchin, ND '81, I spotted Coach DeCicco seated at a table. I introduced myself, wished him a

Happy New Year and told him I looked forward to fencing for him. He graciously smiled and greeted us. Naive or not, I felt this was a sign I had made the right choice to participate in Fencing.

The atmosphere in the fencing gym was magical for me. I improved quickly and competed in the Great Lakes Fencing Championships in 1979 after being trained by Michael Sullivan, ND '79, Dodee Carney, Sharon Moore and

Coach DeCicco, as well as many teammates in the fencing gym.

When I informed Coach that as a Fine Art Major I would attend the SMC Rome Program in Italy for my sophomore year, Coach offered to contact Club Scherma Roma and Michele Maffei, Olympic gold and silver medalist, so my training could continue. Every Tuesday possible, I took the city bus from Chiesa II Gesu to Stadio Olimpico for fencing lessons from an Italian Maestro and trained with one of the premier women's fencing programs in the world at that time. Coach, Polly and their son Michael invited Michael Molinelli, ND '82, and me to meet them in Venice, Italy, the Spring of 1980 for the Junior World Fencing Championships for a couple of days to cheer for team USA. Coach's influence so far from home filled me with gratitude and determination to return to SMC/ND my junior year ready to contribute toward a successful season.

In 1981, a Hungarian woman, Gina Farkashazy, from Wayne State was the woman to beat. I defeated her twice, once during a regular season match and again for 1st Place at Wisconsin-Parkside hosting the Great Lakes Fencing Championships. It was my chance to thank Coach DeCicco for all his generosity and to defeat his nemesis, Wayne State. My captain, Sharon Moore, told me right before my championship match with Gina that Coach had declared in the captain's meeting the night before, "Twila has the attitude capable of winning this whole thing." True or not, I believed every word. Coach was standing nearby, between Maestro Istvan Danosi of Wayne State and Charlotte Remenyik, head coach of Ohio State. They were frowning and Coach was smiling. In addition to St. Mary's College Women's Team finishing first, I claimed 1st place individually. As a side note, when ND Women's Fencing statistics are posted in the annual ND Fencing Program, Coach kept the ND vs. SMC record intact, 0-2 from 1980-1982. Sadly SMC discontinued the Varsity Fencing team in the late 1980s.

Maybe Coach DeCicco has a sixth sense for student athletes praying for guidance. My father, T. Mark Kitchin, Jr., was severely injured and permanently brain damaged from an automobile accident in 1973. My father's favorite university had been Notre Dame, and Saint

Mary's at Notre Dame offered a Nationally Accredited BFA degree. I knew where my father would want me to pursue my undergraduate education. My brother Mark and I followed our father's excitement for Notre Dame. My father was no longer physically able to participate in my life, but spiritually he was a driving force. When my mother, Barbara Kitchin, faced health issues during my senior year, Coach knew I was anxious to go home to be with her during spring break. He saw my frustration with my senior year results, finishing 5th at the 1982 Great Lakes Championships, less successful than junior year. Coach met with me before I went home. I thanked him for everything he had done for me. I was sad to be done with college fencing, but I looked forward to helping my mother recover from surgery. Coach told me fencing should not be my first priority, and that my priorities were correct.

According to my husband of 28 years, Joe Mulflur, Jr. ND '82, a Notre Dame pole vaulter, I dashed across his path many times on the pole vault runway at the ACC. In order to go to the fencing gym location at that time from the athlete's locker rooms, crossing the indoor track area and specifically the pole vault pit was a daily occurrence. We finally met our senior year in the spring. It's a story we enjoy telling our 4 children, Joe III, Matt, Twila and Peter.

Coach DeCicco guided many student athletes with an uncanny sense of well-timed words of encouragement and direction. He told me during fencing lessons that I had a sense of timing that was exceptional. What I lacked in years of experience and sometimes discipline was over-come with enthusiasm. Coach DeCicco celebrated a fencer's strengths while helping improve their weaknesses. The last touch was all that mattered—a fencer's ability to summon their attributes and leave it all on the strip, dripping with sweat and exhaustion.

      Twila Kitchin Mulflur
      Saint Mary's College at Notre Dame '82 - fencing

Simply put, I graduated from ND because of the fencing team and the monogram club. It is time I paid my dues and make sure others have the same opportunity available to them.

Starting out at ND, I struggled in my classes and switched majors at will. When I became involved with fencing and then realized that winning the coveted jacket might not happen due to my grades, my outlook changed. Of course, having to sit down with Coach DeCicco and face the embarrassment of having disappointed him also help put me on the straight and narrow. I began to realize that I was wasting my God-given talents, both on and off the strip. All my life I had been the proverbial straight-A student and strong athlete. Those traits had always complemented each other and helped me be successful in all aspects of my life—and helped strengthen my relationship with God. When I saw that my status on the team was in jeopardy, and then having to face the shame of disappointing my coach...well, let's just say that some prayer time at the Grotto got me back on track. I went from probation to Dean's List from one semester to the next. I went on to be part of a team that won the National Championship and graduated with my BA and went on to earn a MBA from another institution. In later years, I married a wonderful woman and we are raising two little domers.

The support of my coach and team, and my desire to remain a part of that community, was core to why I made it at ND. And that success and sense of community has stayed with me and helped guide me since I graduated.

In the end, wearing my ring and my jacket was a life-changer for me. I must admit my jacket is too tight and now hangs near my father's monogram jacket from Loyola, but I wear the ring every day of my life.

Michael A. Bathon '86 - fencing

As a 1953 freshman, I read (on a Farley Hall bulletin board) an invitation to join the fencing team—which I did, and I was given a foil. Walter Langford, a highly respected professor in the College of Arts and Letters, who had no personal fencing experience, was the coach of the Notre Dame fencing team at the time. The following year Mike DeCicco, with considerable fencing experience, especially in sabre, made a major difference to the overall capability of a Notre Dame team which had been rather inferior to the East Coast teams.

I had arrived as a 16-year-old freshman from France via Quebec City. In those years, integrating into a university class essentially composed entirely of Americans was not easy. The fencing team made my integration into Notre Dame life possible. And more so than any other person, Mike DeCicco was my facilitator. Later, in 1957, when an injury caused me to forfeit a number of bouts at the NCAA tournament, Mike DeCicco was again the man of the hour for me in that sad and painful event.

I'm not very far from my 80 years of life. I've fondly remembered Mike DeCicco all these· years. Needless to say it...I am not now likely to forget this exceptional man!

Pierre du Vair '57 - fencing

A NOTRE DAME MAN

Mike had a profound impact on my academic career without ever having spoken with him. As a freshman I went to his office during the third week of school to ask him if I could drop a class. I was finding that schoolwork was occupying way too much time and was interfering with my football pursuits. As I took a seat in the waiting room I looked to my left and noticed that Mike's office door was ajar enough that I could clearly hear voices and witness a life-changing event.

Mike had crossed swords mounted on the wall behind his desk, I assumed as a symbol of his affection for fencing. Within two minutes of my entering the waiting room, Mike jumped up from his desk, grabbed one of the swords off the wall and pointed it at the throat of my nameless teammate and yelled, "If you cut one more class, I'll take care of you with this rusty saber!" At that time I realized that academics at Notre Dame were a priority. That was the only motivation I needed. I quickly exited the Administration Building and went directly to the library without Mike knowing I had been there.

Ken MacAfee '78 – football

The first time I met coach DeCicco, it was short and sweet. Al l of the freshmen athletes were shuttled into a room immediately after reporting for our first year on campus. Coach got up in front of the group and told all what was expected of us while attending the University of Notre Dame. He told us that it was a special place and that "wanting a challenge" was part of the reason that we came to the university.

Mandatory study hall was going to be required for the first semester, until he could see that we were responsible for attaining higher academic standings. Non-attendance of classes would not be tolerated. There were no excuses.

Then we broke up into groups and waited to receive our first semester book lists. It was here that the first one-on-one contact with coach DeCicco took place. Eye contact was made,

I spoke my name to him, and then he made the indelible comment, "I saw your SAT scores. You're a Mental Midget in spite of your size."

"Mental Midget?" Me? Needless to say, the comment fired me up. My SAT score was darned good.

But looking back I can see that his comment was made to ensure that I kept a higher academic level than would be expected. By uttering that challenge, he dared me to progress on a higher plane to graduation.

After 4 years and a group of Dean's List postings, I graduated with honors from ND. In addition to many hours of sheltering at the Library while doing my readings, there is no doubt that the initial challenge made by Coach DeCicco got me off to a running start towards graduation. His bit of psychology went a long way.

George Kunz '69 - football

A NOTRE DAME MAN

I remember a meeting held in Coach DeCicco's office after midterm grades were posted sophomore year and I was called in. Soon after my arrival, fellow classmates Tom Fine, Mike Fanning and Sherman Smith appeared. All had a meeting scheduled with DeCicco at the same time as mine. We were escorted into his office and there he stood—beet red and holding a sword. We sat and his lecture went something like this: "Here sits the 2 F's and the 2 S's, Fine, Fanning, Sylvester and Smith, a disgrace to the University. He slammed his sword against his desk inches from my nose with a loud crack and then hate spewed from his mouth describing what would happen unless we started studying. We were pushed out the door and were told never to come back. Great guy. Smart guy. Big temper!

Steve Sylvester '75 - football

I am sure people recall many of the "sayings" of
Coach D. But the one that has stayed etched in my mind
for years is: "Know what you want to do, and do it!" I
remember as a freshman laughing at this advice because
it really didn't tell you anything specific while you
were out there on the fencing strip. But as I have
reflected on it over the years, the saying turns out to
be great words to live by.

Mike van der Velden '86 - fencing

My path to ND fencing was atypical—I learned to fence in the PE program my freshman year. After winning the NVA tournament, I met Coach DeCicco and learned about ND's "novice" tradition. I found a fencing club near my home that summer and prepared to try to make the team my sophomore year. The season began with a picnic at Coach's home. I was astonished to see this legendary man open his home to us; this was my first view into ND fencing and I was so excited. He and his wife Polly could not have been nicer. I quickly learned that this would not be my "sport," my "activity" or even my "team."
This was a family.

Despite the fact that I was not an extraordinary fencer (my career record was only 16-3), Coach always made me feel like I was truly part of the team, and that my growth and success were as important to him as to the myriad All-Americans on squad. He always took time to instruct not just about fencing but about how to treat others and how to make our way through life. I was even fortunate enough my senior year to receive a sabre lesson from him; a memory I'll cherish forever.

The most important thing I learned from Coach (other than some colorful phrases about the various uses for a rusty sabre) was to treat all people with kindness regardless of their state or status. As a novice on the team I expected to be relegated to second-tier status. Instead, I always felt included as part of the team and learned a great deal that I keep with me as I go through life.

Jim Kowalski '89 - fencing

·When I arrived at Notre Dame in the fall of 1965, I was all of 5'6" and 120 lbs. I had never participated in any organized sports, much less fencing (although I played a lot of sandlot and pick-up baseball, softball, football and basketball). Early in the spring semester of my freshman year, I noticed signs around campus advertising the fencing team. They featured the message: "No experience necessary." Well, I thought, I meet the first requirement anyhow. So I decided to try it. To keep the rest of the story short, I went out, practiced, and did reasonably well in the freshman tournament. I stuck with the team, earning a monogram and having a great time in the process. I also put on about 30 pounds of much-needed weight. I have some great memories from my years on the team, and will be eternally grateful to Coach for having had the opportunity to compete for the Fighting Irish. Contrary to popular conception, fencing is the best team on campus! I continued to compete in fencing through my 40s. It has been a wonderful ride.

Thanks, Coach.
Mike Schnierle - '69 fencing

ABOUT THE AUTHOR

Jeremy D. Bonfiglio is the Features Writer for The Herald-Palladium *newspaper in Saint Joseph, Michigan. In a 21-year journalism career, he's also held features and sports writing staff positions at newspapers in Indiana, Ohio, Colorado, California, Wyoming and Arizona.*

As a freelance writer Bonfiglio's work has appeared in Notre Dame Magazine, The Writer, Chicago Tribune, Arizona Republic, Fort Worth Star-Telegram, Rocky Mountain Sports and American Hockey magazine. This is his first book.

Bonfiglio is a Centerville, Ohio, native, and a graduate of Eastern Kentucky University. He lives in South Bend, Indiana, with his wife, Karyn, and their son, William.